MORALITY WITHIN
THE FRAMEWORK OF REALITY

Providing a Realistic Framework for
Human Thought and Behavior

LISA JOHNSON

ISBN- 979-8-9917775-0-6

Second Edition

Dedicated to my friend beyond the sea
who is lovingly guiding me home.

CONTENTS

Rulers

The rulers wanted to fool us,
since they saw we were connected with the good.
They took the names of the good
and gave them to the not good.
So with names they could trick
and rope us to the not good.
As though doing us a favor,
they took names from the not good
and placed them on the good
They knew what they were doing.
They wanted to grab those of us who were free
and make us eternal slaves.

From the Gnostic Gospel of Phillip

The Divinity of Evil

They cracked the code that gives us life.
The God they killed makes them divine.
The beasts of destruction sit on the throne
of the barren planet they made our home.

They will choose who lives and dies.
They will choose who works and thrives.
Within the algorithm choice is stored;
the leaden tomb of either/or.

Lisa Johnson

INTRODUCTION

S tudying Adolf Hitler and the holocaust, after studying the Bible and Jesus in terms of the human mind, rather than in terms of the academic and religious teachings of my youth, has taught me that what we label as good and evil is not an either/or proposition; although we may like to think otherwise when faced with a merciless killer like Adolf Hitler. All one has to do is view photos of the starved, corpse-like figures of human beings that inhabited the concentration camps and read about the horrors of the medical experiments done in those camps to conclude that Hitler and the people who enabled him like Dr. Josef Mengele, Heinrich Himmler and Adolf Eichmann were evil monsters. And that is exactly what I did when I saw the photos and heard about the experiments. It was easy to view Hitler as Satan himself because to do otherwise would have required me to wrap my head around how skeletal and starved mountains of human bodies could just be disposed of like trash.

Ironically enough, what I have discovered is that Hitler had his own ideas about the satans and evil monsters of our world. When writing about Marxism and the Social Democratic movement of his day in his personal memoir titled, *Mein Kampf,* he wrote the following:

"It must be admitted that the original authors of this evil [Marxism] which has infected the nations were <u>devils</u>

incarnate. For only in the brain of a monster, and not that of a man, could the plan of this organization take shape whose workings must   finally bring about the collapse of human civilization and turn this world into a desert waste."[1]

Later in the book, Hitler claimed that it was not until finding out the 'original authors' of Marxism were not only the evil devils of this world, but Jewish as well, that he was transformed from being a "soft-hearted cosmopolitan to an out-and-out anti-Semite."[2] His transformed, anti-Semite mind then concluded that if the Jew, with the aid of his Marxist creed, were to triumph over the people of the world, it would spell the end of mankind itself.[3] It was then that his mission in life became clear to him. He had to rid the world of the the Jew in order to save mankind itself; believing that doing so was in accordance with the will of the Almighty Creator because it was "in standing guard against the Jew that he would be defending the handiwork of the Lord."[4]

There is a lot to unpack in Hitler's belief that he was defending the handiwork of God. Hitler goes from A to Z in saying that since a Jew, namely Karl Marx, authored the philosophy known as Socialism and a number of Jews believed in and propagated the Socialist agenda as represented by the Social Democratic Party in Germany at the time, then it was his responsibility to eradicate them all before they were able to destroy mankind itself. It did not occur to him that many non-Jews were Marxists as well (a/k/a Social Democrats), nor did he back up his belief with any evidence of how exactly mankind would be destroyed either by the Socialist creed or by any Jew who was a Socialist. Like so many authoritarians before and after him who do not have facts to back them up, Hitler relied on good old God as his justification to cause all the destruction he eventually exacted on the world.

It was obviously an irrational and tortured thought process that got his mind to thinking it was a righteous goal to kill millions of people as a means for saving humanity. Hopefully, I will be able to explain in this book the catalyst behind his thinking process. But first, I think we all must question whether the God of creation would ever choose the destructive act of killing to achieve its vision because it is not only Hitler who used God and the concepts of good and evil to justify killing and war. It is many of us. I think Hitler's anti-Semite mindset and my own prior mindset that viewed him as the Devil incarnate proves that what we label as good and evil in this physical world we inhabit is purely a subjective concept created in the mind of the individual human being.

Nazism, more than anything else, was a set of corrupted thought patterns inflicted on a society by one man who had the knowledge, power and means for doing so. He laid out his methods in his autobiography, *Mein Kampf*, and then executed them with mathematical precision so that his agenda would be carried out without opposition. The agenda could only be carried out by a populace that had their minds corrupted through pressure, propaganda, fear, punishment and all the other methods used by Hitler to get them to conform to the agenda.

However, make no mistake about it. These patterns of thinking and behavior are not confined to Nazi Germany. They are found throughout the history of mankind in environments as small as a family and as big as the global world stage. They have harmed the consciousness and lives of individual human beings since we became a species and unless they are identified and rooted out from their source in the individual human mind, they will continue to wield their destructive force among our fellow men and women into future generations.

The only difference between us and someone like Adolf Hitler, whom I talk about extensively in this book as a master of illusion, is that Adolf Hitler perfected the processes for creating illusion on a grand scale, so that millions of people fell under its corrupting spell. Since most people consider Hitler and his regime as one of the most evil in human history, this book seeks to identify patterns of thought that manifested in outward behavior in Nazi Germany so that we can begin decoding the illusion of evil and become more grounded in the positive vibrations of truth and reality.

If we were to identify these thought patterns, we could prevent them from manifesting themselves in outward behavior. Historically, the task of identifying these patterns of thought has been relegated to religion and unfortunately the world's major religions have done much to encourage wrong behavior, or what they would term *evil* behavior, by not openly discussing its root causes. By placing their prophets on a pedestal and placing the messages of Muhammed, Jesus, Buddha in a realm called *spirit*, rather than grounding their messages in human nature where they belong, evil has been allowed to fester and grow like the mutant virus it is.

In this book, I choose to do away with the words *good* and *evil* as much as possible because those words have been hijacked by religion and religion has no place in this book. In this book, I will deal with cold, hard facts and reality without the labels that religion has given them. Although I will do away with religion, I will incorporate some facts and truth provided to us from Jesus and the Bible, as I do in all my works. Even though both Jesus and the Bible have been hijacked by the institution called religion, the universal truths and knowledge they meant to convey belong to all mankind regardless of religion.

Jesus has a central role in this book because his was the voice of truth. As the voices of truth are becoming louder and louder in our present day and the numbers of people speaking it are increasing exponentially, the power hierarchies around the world are employing the strategies of the mob to silence them. They are killing the messengers, arresting the truth tellers and harassing the non-conformists. Technology is working in their favor, and my fear is that many truth tellers like Jesus will have to make very difficult decisions in favor of retaining their consciousness of truth in a world that is upside-down as a result of believing that secrecy and deception will rescue it when the opposite is true. It is leading to its destruction.

I prefaced this book with a section titled "Rulers" from the Gnostic Gospel of Phillip. It basically says that the rulers of this world had to turn the tables on God, or what we have traditionally considered righteous and good in our Judeo-Christian society, in order to seize control of our minds and make us believe that what is not good is good.

It is amazing to me that a man like Hitler was ever allowed into a position of power and once there, not exposed for being the master illusionist he was in turning the not good into the good, and then getting an army of bystanders and enablers to help him spread the mind virus to masses of people. As he himself said in Mein Kampf, there is a very methodical process for doing this that he learned from studying the Social Democrats (Communists) of his day and he employed every tactic in the book to seize control of the minds of the German people and make them think that what was good was not good and what was not good was good.

My goal in writing this book is to give individuals the same knowledge Hitler and the author of the Gospel of Phillip had. I hope I am able to show that the man we have labeled as the most evil in the world was using age-old tactics of mind corruption that rulers before him used and that rulers since him have continued to use to further their agendas and retain their power and control over the masses. I want to expose how these illusionists corrupt a person's mind because no matter how corrupt a society becomes, it is the individual human being who is ultimately responsible for the decisions they make. We are the rulers of our own destinies, based upon what we know to be true about ourselves, and it is our responsibility to act in accordance with truth and not with what somebody else tells us is true.

In order to keep our minds grounded in what we know to be the true and the good, we each must come to an understanding of reality by accepting facts and only facts as the starting off point for all our decisions. That is what living in truth entails and if the rulers are successful in making us believe the good is not the good, then you can readily see how living in truth becomes extremely difficult.

I want people to understand the mind of Adolf Hitler as well as the minds of the people that were corrupted into believing the not good of Nazi ideology was good. As much as we want to believe it would never happen to us on a collective level, much less an individual level, the truth is it happens to us all the time in our daily lives if we are not vigilant in watching our emotions and thoughts at all times and making certain they are aligned with what is true. In separating ourselves from men and women like Hitler by labeling them as evil and refusing to look any further into their motivations and thought processes, we have opened ourselves up to continued victimization at their hands because the lessons to be learned are not from how different Hitler's mind was from the rest of us. Rather, they are to be found in how similar it was and how each of us can fall into the same traps he did if we are not vigilant in the thoughts we entertain and the emotions we choose to engage.

PART I - ILLUSION

CHAPTER 1
The Formation of Hitler's World View

A person's world view is usually shaped early in life based upon one's upbringing, education and environment. Unless a trauma or other life-changing event happens to cause a person to alter that world view, it will usually remain the same throughout life. Although it is easy to call Hitler evil and leave it at that, the fact is he was a human being. Like the rest of us, his world view was shaped largely by environmental influences and personal experiences that took place early in his life.

Hitler was born in Braunau-on-the-Inn, a small town on the border of Austria and Germany. According to *Mein Kampf*, Hitler decided at age twelve that he wanted to be an artist. When he told his father about his career aspirations, he was met with resistance. It had always been his father's dream for young Adolf to pursue a career in governmental civil service just as he did. However, Adolf had dreams of his own. To him, the idea of going into governmental service was horrifying, just as it would be to most any young, aspiring artist. As Hitler writes in *Mein Kampf*, becoming a civil servant was something that "no power in the world could force me to become."[5] Therefore, whenever his father would voice his objections about his son becoming an artist, Hitler would become even stronger in his conviction to pursue that path. When his father wouldn't budge on his objections to his son's desire to become an artist, young Adolf decided he would rebel against his father's wishes by only studying in school the subjects that most appealed to him and neglect the others. Later on, as I will show, that strategy backfired on him in a big way. It altered Hitler's future and changed the trajectory of his life toward the career he hated so much and his father so desired for him.

In terms of personality, Hitler was both obstinate and headstrong. Those qualities served him well in achieving his goals. However, those same traits caused him to behave in ways that worked to his detriment throughout his life and may very well have cost him the war when he refused to budge in his decisions, even when experts were giving him excellent advice to the contrary. Years after the war, when Joachim von Ribbentrop, Minister of Foreign Affairs of Nazi Germany from 1938 to 1945, testified at his trial at Nuremberg, he said that he felt like he was facing a man who knew what he wanted and who had an unshakable will and a very strong personality.[6] I would say that Ribbentrop's observation was fairly accurate based on Hitler's own assessment of himself in *Mein Kampf.*

Although Hitler doesn't say it in the book, it is my own opinion that his father opposed his son's decision to become an artist as strongly as he did out of a sense of love. His father grew up in poverty and civil service provided him with a good standard of living. He did not want his son to suffer as he had. As with most adolescents, Hitler did not see it that way at all, so all the friction and arguments between father and son continued until Hitler's father died when Hitler was thirteen years old. Shortly after his father's death, his mother became seriously ill and all the money he would have inherited from his father's estate was spent on medical bills for his mother.

In the final years of his mother's illness and just before her death, Hitler applied to the Academy of Fine Arts in Vienna. Although the admissions officials at the Academy thought Hitler had talent, they rejected his application based upon their opinion that he was not suited for painting. When he spoke to the Rector of the school about it, he was told that his sketches indicated he may have an aptitude for architecture, and he was encouraged to apply to the School of Architecture. Although Hitler talked himself into thinking he would be a very good architect, his failure to graduate middle school because of the decision he made years earlier to neglect some of his studies precluded his admission into the School of Architecture.

Adolf Hitler was only sixteen years old when his mother died. In quick succession, he became homeless, traveled alone to Vienna, was rejected from Art School and found himself unable to attend Architecture School. Essentially, he was alone in Vienna with his dreams dashed, no job, the lack of a middle school certificate, grieving the death of his mother and with no family to whom he could turn to for support. As he described it in *Mein Kampf*, Hitler lived the next five years of his life alone in a strange city - often hungry and depressed and with only his books for company.

When not doing odd jobs as a painter and laborer, he was reading. It was during his life in Vienna that Hitler's world view was fully formed and a "definite outlook on the world took shape" in his mind.[7] In his words, it was during that time that his eyes were opened to two perils: Marxism and Judaism. However, it was not all the reading he did that brought these two perils together in his mind. Rather, it was an experience that happened to him during that very vulnerable time in his existence that filled him with an obsessive hatred for Social Democracy (Marxism) and for the Jews who he saw as its chief promoters.

When one is hungry and destitute, a job is a necessity. It is the means for one's survival and so at seventeen years of age, Hitler was able to acquire a job in the building trade. It was there where he came into contact with colleagues who were Social Democrats. Before that time, Hitler claimed that Marxism was very little known to him and that his only acquaintance with the Social Democratic Party was as a spectator at some of their mass meetings. When he heard his Social Democratic work colleagues talking politics at lunch while he ate a sandwich alone in the corner, he was filled with inner disgust because building tradeeverything they said was counter to his own views on nationalism and his patriotic devotion to the 'fatherland'.[8] He felt like his Social Democratic colleagues disparaged all the ideas he loved. Hitler wrote that they viewed nationalism as an invention of the capitalist class and they hated the concept of *the Fatherland* because it was used as an instrument of the bourgeoisie for the exploitation of the working class. Additionally, they hated authority in the form of the law because it was used as a means of holding down the masses and they hated religion because it was used as a means to dope the people so as to exploit them later. In Hitler's mind, there was nothing good in this world that the Social Democratic Marxists did not drag through the mud.[9]

After a while, Hitler could no longer stay silent in the corner eating his lunch alone and so he began to engage with them to counter everything they said. In his interactions with his work colleagues, Hitler's obstinacy once again reared its ugly head to Hitler's own detriment. He would spend all his off hours from work devouring every book and pamphlet he could find on Social Democracy so that he could win all the arguments he was getting into with his co-workers.[10] However, instead of admiring his vast knowledge of the subject as he had expected them to do, his colleagues got very angry with him and began intimidating him and getting into actual physical altercations with him. The admiration he expected from them became his doom when they instead viewed him as an instigator and troublemaker deserving of banishment from 'their' workplace. Eventually, they had him fired and literally threw him out on the street.

He describes the aftermath of his job termination as follows:

"When my anger began to calm down the spirit of obstinacy got the upper hand and I decided that at all costs I would get back to work again in the building   trade.   This   decision became all the stronger a few weeks later, when my little savings had entirely run out and hunger clutched me once again in its merciless arms. <u>No alternative was left to me. I got work again and had to leave it for the same reasons as before. Then I asked myself: Are these men worthy of belonging to a great people?</u> The question was profoundly disturbing; for if the answer were "Yes", then the struggle to defend one's nationality is no longer worth all the trouble and sacrifice we demand of our best elements if it be in the interests of such a rabble. On the other hand, if the answer had to be "No" – these men are not worthy of the nation", then our nation is poor indeed in men. <u>During those days of mental anguish and deep meditation I saw before my mind the ever-increasing and menacing army of people who could no longer be reckoned as belonging to their own nation.</u>"[11]

As the above passage states, no sooner had Hitler obtained a second job and he was fired from it for the same reason as the first. He had just been fired from two jobs for being perceived among his work colleagues as an agitator and troublemaker. It is clear from this passage that Hitler despised his workplace colleagues for doing what they did to him. However, he seemed to be incapable of separating the men's actions from their ideology. Although he had a right to his own political opinions, he probably should have kept them to himself in the workplace. However, losing one's job is always a traumatic experience no matter the reason given, particularly when one is young, alone, hungry and financially desperate. Anxiety, anger, depression and the sense of hopelessness and helplessness that go along with it has the effect of fogging the mind and I think it is clear that Hitler's mind is fogged when he concludes that the men who had him fired, and all men like them holding the same political views, *have no place in the nation*. Through his fogged and scattered thinking process, Hitler thereby made his termination not only as an affront to himself, but to the entire nation. More than obstinacy though, I think it was his extremely strong ego exerting itself into the process.

Although this passage shows that it was Hitler's soul and mind that was injured as a result of the unjust firing as manifested in his mental anguish and depression, it was his ego that was crushed because his colleagues would not acknowledge his point of view in any way, shape or form.

I think it could be argued that Hitler wasn't so much interested in discussing a differing point of view with his workplace colleagues when he studied his books so hard in his off hours; as it was a matter of very much wanting to win the argument. Unfortunately for him, the men with whom he engaged in the arguments at work wanted the win as well. The difference between the two parties is that the men at work had the power to throw him out on the street. With his firing, he lost the argument in a big way.

It was at that point in time he decided he would never lose the argument again and he became obsessed with learning everything he could about the Social Democratic method for winning. Toward that end, he wrote the following in *Mein Kampf*:

"Within less than two years I had gained a clear understanding of Social Democracy, in its teaching and the technique of its operations. I recognized the infamy of that technique whereby the movement carried on a campaign of mental terrorism against the bourgeoisie, who are neither morally nor spiritually equipped to withstand such attacks. The tactics of Social Democracy consisted in opening, at a given signal, a veritable drum-fire of lies and calumnies against the man whom they believed to be the most redoubtable of their adversaries, until the nerves of the latter gave way and they sacrificed the man who was attacked, simply in the hope of being allowed to live in peace. But the hope proved always to be a foolish one, for they were never in peace. The same tactics are repeated again and again, until fear of these mad dogs exercises, through suggestion, a paralysing effect on their Victims."[12]

Although Hitler hated the Social Democrats personally, he very much admired their tactics. In his rise to power, Hitler assiduously studied the strategies of the Social Democrats. Learning their techniques was a way for him to win the advantage. It is a classic example of the bullied becoming the bully – the abused becoming the abuser in the cycle of abuse. As counter intuitive as it may sound, a crushed ego is probably the seed contained within every psychopathic mindset. And make no mistake about it. Adolf Hitler's mindset was very much what has been labeled as psychopathic.

As a result of his extensive research into Marxism, Hitler came to three conclusions: (1) the Marxists knew how to create a mass movement, without which any political party was useless; (2) they had learned the art of propaganda among the masses; and, (3) they knew the value of using what he called "spiritual and physical terror."[13] Hitler's conclusion that men like the men he argued with at work are an "ever-increasing and menacing army of people who could no longer be reckoned as belonging to their own nation" because of the opinions they held was clearly not a rational view, and the fact that he held that view until the end of his days is a testament to his self-proclaimed obstinacy. The fact that a psychopath was put into power with full knowledge of his views on display in his writings is a testament to our human inclination to believe what we want and totally disregard what is in plain sight.

Hatred and anger certainly played a role in Hitler's irrational belief that the Social Democrats had no place in the country, but so also did his views on nationalism itself. Hitler was nationalistic from a very young age because of his father. However, Hitler's version of nationalism did not comport with how most people view it. Also, it did not comport with the dictionary definition of nationalism. The Merriam-Webster dictionary defines nationalism as "loyalty and devotion to a nation; especially a sense of national consciousness exalting one nation above all others and placing primary emphasis on promotion of its culture and interests as opposed to those of other nations or supranational groups."

To Hitler, nationalism had nothing to do with devotion to a nation itself, but rather, it was devotion to a nationality [of people]. There is a huge difference. Hitler was more interested in the kind of people who comprised a nation, rather than the culture, rules and interests of a nation that made it distinct from other nations. He held a view of nationalism that focused on the physical inhabitants of a nation rather than the ideas that underpin a nation. It was his strong views on this kind of nationalism that justified his later actions of rounding up and putting into concentration camps different groups of people he decided could no longer be reckoned with as belonging to their own nation. Those groups included Social Democrats and Jews, as well as "political prisoners, anti-socials, gypsies, felons, homosexuals, and, before 1937, also the Bible-researchers."[14]

As one can ascertain from his writings, Hitler did not consider himself evil in the least. He considered himself strong and right in his convictions. He saw the tactics of the Social Democrats as an effective means for gaining the win for his ideology, just as the men in his workplace got their win by getting rid of the dissenter and troublemaker so that they could all be in communion with their Marxist ideas.

It was most certainly Hitler's ideology that gave the world the human targets of the holocaust, but it was the Marxist tactics he used that allowed it to succeed. Hitler used Marxist propaganda and terror techniques because they worked with "mathematical certainty in destroying one's adversaries."[15] It was never a matter of good and evil to Hitler, no matter how much he proclaimed in all his speeches that God was directing him in his mission to save humanity. It was always a matter of winning at any cost and his use of God was a means to an end of winning.

As Hitler says over and over again in *Mein Kampf,* he was an avid reader. Hitler loved his books, especially those written by his adversaries so he could learn their mindset and thereby gain an advantage. I cannot help but think that if young Adolf was alive today, his bookshelf would be filled with books like *The 48 Laws of Power* and *The Art of War.* These books tell you not to think in terms of right and wrong, positive and negative. Instead, they tell you to be strategic in how you play the game. If you play the game well, you will not get burned. It is partly due to the popularity of these books and countless other books like them that the patterns of thought and behavior that were so roundly condemned by the Allies at the Nuremberg trials have become an acceptable means for silencing perceived enemies, obtaining conformance of the populations and gaining a competitive advantage in our highly technological and networked world. In fact, I would be willing to bet that almost every one of the CEO and managerial controllers in our current corporate and governmental structures of power has a copy of the *Art of War* and the *48 Laws of Power* on their book shelves because those are two of the most popular playbooks used for winning the game of power and control.

At the core of competitive systems fighting for supremacy (whether it be an individual, a business or a country) is the idea that we must keep our strategies close to the cuff for fear that if we give them away, we lose our competitive edge. The end result of such conditioning is that systems are created that require more and more deception and secrecy for their survival. The winners take all in these systems and the winners are the ones who can play the system best. Unfortunately, the people who play the systems best are rarely the best people. More often than not, they are narcissistic, cutthroat and unaware human tools playing a game they make it their life's goal to win. That is what happens when you pit human being against human being in systems built on foundations of competition and hierarchy rather than cooperation and teamwork.

I think the most astonishing fact I learned from reading the transcripts of the Nuremberg trials is how few men it took to take over a country and turn it into a hell on earth with the consent and cooperation of the populace. That takeover would have been impossible without the tactics Hitler learned from the Social Democrats and that he used to conform the minds of a population that was not at all well versed in them. Hitler and his goons had the advantage in the power game and it allowed the very few to control the hearts, minds and bodies of the millions of people over which they stole control with the tactics learned from the Social Democrats.

I hope to identify some of the patterns of thought that result in what the Bible terms as evil behavior and what Hitler defined as strength. The reason they were transformed from thought patterns into strategies is because they are very effective in obtaining the win on a mass scale. They are the strategies for creating illusion so that incipient patterns of mind corruption can slip under the radar with the propaganda that says the good is the not good and the not good is the good. Hitler used these strategies to great effect in corrupting the minds of the population who were daily subjected to his propaganda and, as I later discuss, it is what the Pharisaic chief priest did to all the people who stood by as an innocent man named Jesus was railroaded through the court and given over to the Romans so he could be executed on a cross because Pharisaic law did not allow for executions.

Chapter 2
Creating the Illusion

If the truth and reality of a situation doesn't serve one's personal agenda, then controllers of reality like Hitler have to depend on something other than truth to achieve their goals. That something other than truth is called perception of truth because perception can be manipulated, twisted, hidden or even turned completely upside-down and inside-out in order to fool us into believing it is the truth. It is the manner in which controllers turn the not-good into the good and the good into the not-good. Ask any Madison Avenue ad executive – without perception, he would be out of work.

In this book, I refer to the perception of reality and truth as illusion because anything other than truth and reality is an illusion. It simply does not exist and a lot of work and power must be exerted by the manipulators of perception to make us believe it does exist.

Adolf Hitler was a master illusionist. He learned from the Social Democrats that if you want to create an illusion, you have to turn the tables on truth and reality itself. He was well aware that individual human beings have free will and therefore are free to make their own decisions. He also knew that convincing individuals it was their duty to submit to an outside authority to make their decisions for them would require the creation of hierarchies of power. In order to convince individual human beings that they do not have the right to speak their own minds, consensus through political means and peer-to-peer pressure would also need to be created. And finally, in order for truth to be denied in favor of an agenda, propaganda and falsehood must be accepted as truth.

Futurist Marc Goodman wrote, "If you control the code, you control the world."[16] He was talking about Artificial Intelligence, but I believe the same can be said of human beings. Control the illusion and you control this world. The way to control the illusion? Create an external environment where truth and reality seem absurd. Then, when a person acts logically in accordance with facts and truth, it places them outside the norm in comparison to the masses who have conformed their minds to the illusion in order to survive emotionally, financially and physically. That is basically what Hitler did in the external environment of Germany and the countries he invaded. Using the tactics he learned from studying Marxism, he created an illusory environment that allowed him to consolidate his power and make him the sole arbiter of what was considered right and wrong in Germany and the other Nazi-occupied countries.

Hitler may have despised the Social Democrats but he very much admired them for the masters of illusion they were. I place the focus of this book on Adolf Hitler and some of the techniques he learned from the extensive research he did on Marxism. However, if one digs a little deeper one realizes that as effective as the Social Democratic techniques are for gaining and retaining power and control, they did not originate with Marxist theory. They were actually plucked from knowledge the human race has had for thousands of years. They have been the playbook for masters of illusion like Hitler since the beginning of civilization itself.

The thought processes for creating the illusion have been

woven into the human consciousness since the human race became conscious. It is my belief that the writers of the Bible were attempting to get us to recognize them so that we can pull them out of our thinking like weeds before they are able to completely overtake our minds. Later in the book, I take a look at Jesus's teachings through this lens. Jesus was a Jew who was educated in the law and scriptures. Much of his knowledge came from the ancient scriptures that now comprise the Old Testament of the Bible. When I read the Old Testament myself, I am struck at how so many of the stories are good examples of the Social Democratic strategies at work.

As much as we might not like to admit it for fear of humanizing the man the world has come to view as evil itself, Hitler was bullied at work by his colleagues and thrown out on the street for expressing a different opinion from them. It was totally unjust when there are so many more constructive ways to deal with people who disagree with us than to take their livelihoods away from them. That is why all the research done on bullying and mobbing shows how destructive it is to the people who are victims of it. It is behavior that goes against all our natural programming to treat others as we ourselves would like to be treated. It is a toolkit of behaviors employed by power abusers in all walks of life who have corrupted their natural programming so that they can gain an advantage in what they view as a power game consisting of winners and losers.

The behaviors we have labeled as bullying and mobbing are examples of master illusionists at work in our schools, workplaces, governments and homes to gain a perceived advantage. Bullying is the face of what we label as evil in this world because the bully employs a tool kit of human thought and behavior to create the illusion that their human target is the problem, rather than they themselves by creating the illusion. Hitler has become the physical face of evil in this world largely because his corrupted thought process caused him to use the bully's toolkit of human thought and behavior on a mass scale to create the illusion that certain groups of people were not worthy of belonging to the nation.

The human toll of these power abusing behaviors is incalculable and will continue to be incalculable until we disavow them, instead of lauding them as strategies for winning. When we place books like the *The Art of War* in the business section of our bookstores and view it as required reading for our managers and CEOs, we dismiss the fact that the book was written to help win wars. Our homes, workplaces, schools and governments should not be viewed as war zones when, in fact, they are communities of people coming together for a shared goal and purpose.

Chapter 3
Decoding the Illusion

Hitler loved taking the Lord's name in vain by passionately proclaiming that he was doing the work of God. An example was when he was at a meeting with the Austrian Chancellor concerning the future of Austria's sovereignty. Hitler self-righteously told the chancellor that he had an historic mission that he would definitely fulfill because God had destined him to do so and that anyone who was not with him would be crushed.[17] Similarly, while making a speech in his hometown of Linz, he emotionally related to the people gathered there that God called him to be a leader, so that he could restore his homeland to the German Reich.[18]

I am quite certain there were numerous other speeches in which Hitler used God to justify war and the murder of millions of men, women and children. People with the wrong intent love to hide behind the veil of righteousness and Hitler is certainly not the first man to start a war with God as his shield, nor will he be the last. He was just one in a long line of master illusionists to use the Creator of life as the justification for the destruction of life. If he had won the war, his justification would have been viewed as the truth and Hitler himself would have been viewed as the savior of mankind he imagined himself to be in *Mein Kampf.* His reputation as a righteous and great man would have been sealed in the history books by myth makers like the master propagandist in chief, Josef Goebbels, and the world may well have been permanently turned upside-down and inside-out without the means for getting it turned right-side up after the illusion became the reality for all.

Before decoding some of the more effective techniques used in creating an illusion, I would like to begin this section of the book with a very short analysis of the Garden of Eden allegory because it shows us the process for creating the illusion in the human mind.[1] Then I will provide an example of a master illusionist from the Bible's Old Testament who, unlike Hitler, was successful in securing his reputation as a man of God and retaining his label of 'prophet' for posterity, even though he was a cold-hearted and vicious killer who loved to invoke the name of God to justify killing thousands of innocents.

The Process for Creating the Illusion as Illustrated by Eve in the Garden of Eden

The Garden of Eden allegory serves as the prelude to the message of the entire Bible by showing us the process for creating the illusion in the human mind. Without going into a lot of detail about it here, the key take-away of the allegory is that Woman's mind (made in the image of God according to Genesis 1:27) is first corrupted with rationalizations and lies provided to her by the snake before she takes a bite from the forbidden fruit. That mind corruption is necessary in order for her to still feel good about herself after having done something she knows is at variance with the values of the Garden.

---

1   In my book, *The Evolution of Good and Evil*, I give a very detailed analysi of this deeply layered allegory to show that the sin Eve commits in the Garden is not itself the act of eating the fruit. It is the mental process she employs to convince herself it is good to eat the fruit. [Turning the not good into the good] Thought always comes before action. It was the sin of her thought corruption that created the action we label as evil.

Although it doesn't say how she got Adam to take a bite, it most likely was by using the same rationalizations and lies the snake provided to her.

Were they evil for eating an apple they were not supposed to eat? Or did they themselves create what we call evil through the corrupted thought process that gave them the leeway to serve their own needs and desires exclusively, to the detriment of all others, including their own children? If one assumes that paradise resides in staying true to reality in the form of the human consciousness of true and false, then it is the latter.

The allegorical figure representing God gives Woman and Man the opportunity to correct their corrupted thinking by stating the truth of what they did so they can bring their thoughts back into their natural state of alignment. By doing so, the whole of the Garden and its inhabitants would again be protected. However, they refuse to do so. They continue lying and covering up what they with the hope that everyone will just move on. When it comes to universal law, however; there is no such thing as just moving on. The karmic scale of balance must remain balanced.

The God of the Garden represents the karmic scale when it holds their thinking to account. Man and Woman are banned from the Garden in the allegory when they refuse to change their thinking because God knows that the rationalizations and justifications they have adopted into their world views will never again allow them to follow the natural programming they were created with to ensure that the Garden would remain a sustainable, nurturing and positive environment for all its inhabitants. God knew that the Man and Woman he now labeled Adam and Eve were in a state of mind that Jesus called sin that cannot be forgiven. It is, in fact, the same mind corruption the Nazi soldiers had when they incredulously asked news correspondents after the war what it was they had done wrong; and it the same mind corruption Adolf Eichmann had at the time of his arrest when his only concern was for his own family after having destroyed and killed so many hundreds of thousands of other families.

The allegory shows us how the same illusory world created by Woman in the Garden was created by Hitler in Germany. The new versions of the world they both created suited their own self-interests and world views at the expense of reality and truth. In an illusory world, the people in the know of the unwritten rules (illusion) know how to stay safe, while the people kept in the dark who act in alignment with what they perceive to be reality (the written rules supposedly in place) act at their own peril.

The problem with a totalitarian regime like Nazi Germany is that there is a disconnect between the written and unwritten rules in the beginning, but once the dissidents, intellectuals and undesirables are killed off; there is alignment between the corrupt rules and the population that has been coerced into compliance. If they want to hold down a job or otherwise survive in the environment, the options available to them become non-negotiable.

They either conform or suffer the consequences.

Samuel – a Master Illusionist from the Bible's Old Testament

Samuel, an Old Testament prophet, was on a par with Hitler in proclaiming he was doing the work of God when he commanded his protege to kill innocent men, women and children. In I Samuel, Chapter 8, Samuel – who is described as the man who judged Israel – is approached by the elders of Israel asking him to select a king for the nation. Samuel is taken aback that they think they need a king to rule over them and he warns the elders that once they have a king, they will be sorry about their decision. He tells them the king will take their sons and put them in his military; he will make them do his plowing and harvesting; he will make them produce his weapons of war; he will use their daughters as perfumers, cooks, and bakers; he will take their best fields, vineyards, and olive groves, and give them to his servants; he will tax their crops, flocks and grape harvests to give to his officials and his servants; he will take their male and female slaves, as well as their best oxen and donkeys, and use them to do his work and they will become his slaves. Even given these outcomes, Samuel's argument falls on deaf ears. The elders are determined to have their king, so Samuel eventually acquiesces to their demand and begins looking for a king.

After a short search, Samuel decides that a handsome young man named Saul would be a good choice and appoints him as king. Consequently, Saul proves himself in several battles and Samuel is convinced that Saul is the perfect man to use for carrying out a mission Samuel has had in mind for a long time. Soon after, Samuel pulls Saul aside for a friendly chat in which he reminds Saul that it was him, Samuel, who made Saul king after he was instructed to by the Lord. In other words, Samuel is telling Saul, 'You owe me and it would not be a good idea to go against my wishes since God is the one instructing me.' After conversing for a while, Samuel reveals to Saul that God has given him instructions to punish the people of Amalek for what they did in barring the way of the Israelites when they came up from Egypt. He tells Saul to kill the leader of Amalek, along with all the men, women, children and infants, oxen and sheep, camels and donkeys living there. (See I Samuel 15:1-3) To put it another way, Samuel is telling Saul that God is out for revenge against Amalek for what their leader did to the Israelites and that he (God) will settle for nothing less than the lives of every man, woman and child living there. As we will see, it was very much Samuel who wanted revenge.

This is where taking every word in the Bible as the literal word of God has been beyond destructive. Why would we trust that a character named Samuel is expressing God's intent just because he says he is? Don't you think it is more credible to believe that Samuel telling Saul it is the Creator's intention to destroy its creation is an example of how Samuel was attributing his own intent to God just as Hitler did when he told everyone within earshot that it was God's intent for him to save humanity by killing millions of people to create his own deluded vision of how the world should be ordered? If Hitler had won the war, don't you think the history books would have said that Hitler did indeed save humanity and that winning the war was proof that God was backing him?

Religion's view of Samuel as a messenger of God has caused generations of religious leaders and followers to view God as a vengeful God and it has served to turn righteous and good agnostics and atheists against the concept of a Creator altogether. Samuel was a man – a man with an agenda he was too cowardly to pursue himself, so he manipulated others to do his dirty work for him by persuading them it was God's will. In this case it was Saul, who felt very loyal to Samuel for all he perceived Samuel had done for him. It was an easy sell, to say the least.

Both Hitler and Samuel had personal agendas they wanted to fulfill. Unfortunately, they are not the only two people who have said they have a mission from God to fulfill. For millennia, religious and political leaders have claimed to be acting in accordance with God's instructions when they have supported wars and war-like regimes and we human beings have a tendency to fall for it every time. A literal translation of the Bible has helped give these power abusers a pass because they have been backed by people who believe a literal translation of the Bible is the word of God. They have also been backed by a population with the same corrupted processes of thought who believe that there are circumstances where the Creator of life would justify the destruction of life.

Samuel may have been receiving instructions, but they were not from God. They were most likely from the same source that gave Eve the instruction to eat the fruit. Samuel is a power abuser, who like so many power abusers who came before and after him, use God to justify their own blood thirst and corruption. Perhaps that is why the first of the Ten Commandments tells us to respect the God of Creation and not use the name of God to justify any false and destructive purpose (use God's name in vain). Samuel can attribute his desire to have Saul kill an entire community of men, women and infants to God all he wants, but it will never make it so.

In the story, Saul is a warrior. He is a soldier required to follow orders and as the good soldier he is, he follows Samuel's orders and goes into battle against the enemy leader, only he doesn't kill him. He saves him, along with the best of the sheep, oxen and lambs. In other words, Saul makes a judgment call in the heat of battle that violates the instructions Samuel has given him. Poor Saul. Like most people who think it is an admirable quality to be able to think and make good decisions on the fly, he believes he is doing something good by capturing the leader and saving the best animals and that Samuel will be proud of him. He excitedly greets Samuel after the battle saying, "The Lord bless you! I have kept the command of the Lord!" by saving the life of the leader and sparing all the best animals.

Wow, was Saul out in left field on that one. He is totally unaware that the last thing any subordinate should do is disobey the orders of a corrupt authoritarian boss who is too cowardly to examine himself or his motives. Samuel is beside himself with anger at the gall Saul has displayed in not following all his instructions to the letter and -

you guessed it - the Lord comes to Samuel once again telling him, "I regret having made Saul king, for he has turned from me and has not kept my command."

Saul feels really bad for doing what he thought best at the time and he explains to Samuel that he saved the leader and animals out of fear of what the people would do if he did not. Even though Saul had every right to do what he did to protect himself and his soldiers, he feels really bad about disappointing Samuel, who he considers both his friend and mentor. Saul again tells Samuel how sorry he is and offers to return home and worship God with him in order to make amends.

Unfortunately, all the 'I'm sorrys' in the world will never cut it with an egotistical and spiteful authoritarian who is only interested in getting his/her way. They are the centers of the only universe that matters - themselves. When Saul disobeys Samuel and fails to do what he is told by this master of illusion, he becomes no better than the men, women and infants he was ordered to kill. It is only natural that when Saul asks for forgiveness, Samuel again relies on God to blame for his own cold-hearted and callous response, telling Saul, "I will not return with you, because you rejected the word of the Lord and the Lord has rejected you as king of Israel. The Lord has torn the kingdom of Israel from you this day and has given it to a neighbor of yours, who is better than you." Then Samuel asks that Agag, King of Amalek, be brought before him, whereby this self-proclaimed man of God cuts Agag to pieces. Saul and Samuel then go their separate ways and never speak to or see one another again.

The story continues with Samuel angry at himself for ever choosing Saul to be king. His anger is tempered with a healthy dose of fear that Saul will kill him for what he has said and done to him, so he decides to hire a bodyguard and take off to Bethlehem to find Saul's replacement. When Samuel arrives in Bethlehem, word has already reached the town about how Samuel cut King Agag to pieces. His brutal murder of the king has worked in sending the message that no one dare mess with him or his agenda. The cowardly elders have heard the message loud and clear and the Bible describes them as trembling when they greet Samuel and ask him whether or not his visit is a peaceful one.

Samuel replies to the elders saying, "Yes! I have come to sacrifice to the LORD." That exclamation mark is really significant. It shows impatience and embarrassment on his part. The fair and impartial judge has been exposed publicly for the vengeful and cruel human being he is. He has to quickly point out to them that he is there to do something good — that he is a good man who believes in God. He has to reinforce to them that he is a man who does good things in order to erase the reality that he is a self-interested beast who will destroy any individual - mentally, physically or otherwise - to achieve what he personally desires.

After reestablishing his place of honor as a man who does good things, Samuel tells the elders he is in town to choose a new king from among Jesse's eight sons. After Samuel rejects the seven oldest sons, Jesse sends for his youngest son, David, who is outside tending to the family's sheep. Samuel is immediately impressed with the handsome young man and anoints him on the spot as his choice before heading out of town. Personally, I have no doubt that he selects David thinking that the youngest will be the most malleable to his ideas and most adaptable to his orders.

Meanwhile, Saul is back at the palace all but forgotten after Samuel has chosen to 'move on' with his choice for king. Saul is there alone, depressed, confused, humiliated and obsessing over what it is he has done to make Samuel hate him so much. His mentor has abandoned him with no explanation and wanting no further contact with him. The Bible says, "The spirit of the Lord had departed from Saul and he was tormented by an evil spirit from the Lord." With all the confidence he had in his abilities to make good decisions and properly lead a nation shattered and destroyed by a manipulative and lying authoritarian type, Saul is left alone to deal with the pain on his own without knowing why he is having to suffer so much for doing the right thing. I know for a fact that Saul was there frantically going over in his mind every single detail of the conflict with Samuel in an attempt to figure out what he did wrong, what he should have done, what he didn't do, what he could have done, what he would have done differently, what he couldn't have done differently, and on and on and on - day after day after agonizing day.

Sometimes it takes a disinterested party to give a depressed and traumatized person the advice they need. Luckily for Saul, he had servants who cared about him and they are the ones who suggest hiring a harpist to play soothing music for him. However, unbeknownst to Saul, the harpist they suggest happens to be the newly anointed king – David of Bethlehem. Unbeknownst to David, he is about to walk into a hornet's nest in which he is neither psychologically nor emotionally prepared. He is about to become caught up in the cycle of abuse. David is about to face a bully who has himself been bullied. Saul learned his tactics for dealing with human threats from Samuel and he will eventually use them against David when he sees what a good king David will be and how much the people love him. If not for David fleeing to a safe country when he learns that Saul wants to kill him, and only returning upon earing of Saul's death, David would never have become the king of Israel.

The Nazi Ideology

In our modern world, some would label a leader like Samuel a Nazi or Fascist, but it should be made clear that Nazism is not a person or persons as many would have us believe when they throw the word 'Nazi' around to label certain people they don't like and/or with whom they disagree. Nazism is an ideology that was adopted by people because they let their minds fall victim to the false assumptions and beliefs of their authoritarian leader. We all know that Nazism resulted in the killing of millions of Jews, but if you are like me, that is probably the extent of your knowledge. The only book that was required reading in my school was *The Diary of Anne Frank*. In my mind, that limited reading and knowledge of Hitler and Nazi Germany cemented in my mind, and the minds of many others of my generation, that the holocaust was the extent of Nazism. In actuality, the holocaust was the natural end result of the Nazi ideology. It was an ideology that incorporated ancient knowledge about how the human mind works. The Nazi ideology provided the means for creating a frame of mind for achieving a particular end. Hitler couldn't do it on his own. He needed an army of people who thought like he did to achieve his end-goal. The patterns of thought used to create the illusion, which he got from the Marxist Social Democrats, provided him with a very methodical and effective means for conforming the population to his way of thinking.

The Nuremberg trials were the trials held after World War II as a means of holding the surviving German war criminals to account. The transcripts of those trials provide invaluable insight into what those patterns of thought are and how they were used to conform the population into a mindset that would help Hitler achieve his goals. Robert H. Jackson was the chief prosecutor from the United States at the Nuremberg trials. He said that the Reichstag fire, which I discuss later in this book, was set by the Nazi conspirators in order to create a "state of mind." In point of fact, I will show that everything Hitler said and did was manipulated to create a state of mind where his agenda would seem reasonable to the average German citizen. Since his agenda was harmful to large groups of people, he had to convince the masses that it was good and right to think those groups of people deserved the treatment they got. In other words, he had to turn the rules of the democratic and free society that Germany was upside-down to make people believe that the rights of some did not equate to the rights of all. Like the animals in the book *Animal Farm*, Hitler made some people more equal than others using the strategies he learned from studying Communism.

We tend to focus on the fruit eating part of the allegory of Adam and Eve. However, after Eve took a bite from the fruit she had to convince Adam to do the same. How do you think that was done when Adam knew it was wrong to eat the fruit and he didn't have the snake telling him otherwise. All he had was Eve, the new master of illusion in the Garden, convincing him it was right to eat the fruit. How do you imagine she did that? Did she pressure him by telling him she would refrain from sex with him until he did so? Did she repeat the same rationalizations and lies the snake told her to get Adam to eat the forbidden fruit? Did she give him the silent treatment until he gave in? Did she threaten to leave him all alone and childless in the Garden? Did she convince him the world was their oyster if they were united in their wrongdoing? Whatever strategy or strategies she used, they were successful and every last one of them was used by Adolf Hitler in one form or another to get the masses to support him and his agenda.

In the process of researching this book, I learned that all the strategies used by Hitler and the Social Democrats have been used by corrupt authoritarian figures, organizations and regimes since there have been people organized into communities of people. It is unbelievable to me that we have never identified these tactics in order to isolate and destroy them so that they will never be used again to harm another human being. We had all this knowledge from the time the Bible writers wrote about Samuel and Saul and they came into real focus with the treatment of Jesus by the Pharisees. Yet in all my years of going to church when I was young, I have never heard any preacher or pastor preach on them or help their congregation identify them so that they would not have to suffer the same fate as the Jews in Nazi Germany - or Jesus for that matter.

I could write a book on each of the tactics Hitler learned from the Social Democrats as a means for turning the tables on truth and reality; however, for purposes of this book, I have tried to identify a few of them so that we can begin drawing connections and recognizing patterns of thought that cause so much harm to ourselves and our fellow men and women. However, as I have said, these tactics are not exclusive to Hitler. Although I use the first part of this book to show how he incorporated them in his rise to power, the second part of this book shows how the same strategies were used by the Pharisees to control and subjugate the Jewish community and target Jesus when he became too much of a threat in exposing them and the false doctrine they pushed on the community as a means for retaining their power, control and wealth.

Chapter 4
Patterns of the Illusion

The Nuremberg trial transcripts show that the aggressive war plan of the Nazis was thoroughly thought out and reviewed during the years they were making assurances to world leaders that they wanted peace. The plan involved attacking Poland, England, France, the Netherlands and Belgium; all in quick succession. Contained within the transcript is the following excerpt:

> "Following the assurances to the world of peaceful intentions, an influential group of the conspirators met on 23rd May, 1939, to consider the further implementation of their plan. The situation was reviewed and it was observed that "the past six years have been put to good use and all measures have been taken in correct sequence and in accordance with our aims," that the national- political unity of the Germans had been substantially achieved, and that further successes could not be achieved without war and bloodshed. ... It was thereupon determined immediately to prepare detailed plans for an attack on Poland at the first suitable opportunity and thereafter for an attack on England and France, together with plans for the simultaneous occupation by armed force of air bases in the Netherlands and Belgium."[19]

This excerpt shows that Hitler had a plan many years in the making. To the outside world, he promised peace. However, behind closed doors "an influential group of conspirators" met to draw up the details of a plan for invading and occupying countries and establishing bases therein. It should be noted that the prosecutors at Nuremberg had absolutely no problem with using the word 'conspirators' and, in fact, used it and the word 'conspiracy' numerous times throughout the trials to describe the plan and its authors. The following example is just one of many examples where the words conspiracy and conspirators were used to describe Hitler and the people who assisted him in planning his new order of the world behind closed doors:

> "On the contrary, it [the S.A.] was an agency adapted to many designs and purposes; and its role in the conspiracy changed from time to time - always corresponding with the progression of the conspiracy through its various phases towards the final objective: abrogation of the Versailles Treaty and acquisition of the territory of other peoples and nations. If we might consider this as a pattern, with its various parts fitting together like the pieces of a jigsaw puzzle, we would find that the piece representing the S.A. constituted a link in the pattern vitally necessary to the presentation and development of the entire picture."[20]

A conspiracy, by its very nature, is an illusion that is concocted to get around the rules in place. However, Hitler was not a particularly brilliant or even smart man. He didn't come up with an original plan for establishing his new order of power in the world. He resorted to using time-honored patterns of thought and behavior that the Communists of his day became experts at using and the Bible delineates for us throughout with stories like that of Samuel and Saul. However, they came into really clear view when the Pharisee conspirators used just about all of them in their attempts to marginalize, ensnare, capture and crucify Jesus.

The illusionists who use the patterns of illusion are well versed in them and quite conscious of the negative impacts they have on a person's consciousness. The enablers and bystanders they depend on for success are not as knowledgeable and go along with them to stay in the good graces of the orchestrators who plan the entire scenario in secret, behind closed doors. It is time to give those enablers and bystanders the same knowledge the illusionists have so that the choices they make are informed and when held to account, they cannot pass blame and hide behind claims that they were just following orders.

Patterns of the Illusion

1. Lies

Lies destroy truth. They destroy reality itself. Truth provides a foundation for society. A lie destroys that foundation because we cannot make logical and rational decisions that protect ourselves and others based on lies. The lies a politician tells about his opponent's record are meant to get a corrupt person willing to lie into office. The lies a cheating husband tells to his wife are meant to allow him to continue the same corrupt behavior. A person who lies on the witness stand prevents justice from prevailing. Lies our leaders tell prevent other leaders from trusting them and they in turn feel justified in lying back. In all cases, lies support a position, situation, behavior or intent that should not exist in the first place. Each additional lie further supports the illusion and before too long, the world begins to look like a parallel universe where nothing makes sense anymore. That is, until there is no need to lie anymore, which would have been the case if Hitler had been successful in creating his 'new order' and securing it for a thousand years. People would have either conformed or suffered the consequences.[21]

However, getting the new order of the world that Hitler envisioned in place required far more than lies and deception. It also required him to launch aggressive wars while international treaties and agreements were in place.[22] Hitler and his goon squad had to lie to get around those treaties and take over countries. Luckily for them, their ability to lie without any qualms whatsoever came in very handy. Sir Neville Henderson, England's ambassador to Germany from 1937 to 1939, said that he couldn't believe a word Hitler said and added that Hermann Goering, Hitler's Minister of Aviation, lied to him numerous times.[23]

The ability certain people have to lie without blinking an eye or considering who gets hurt by their lies is staggering. The ordinary person who tries to live a good life and lies on occasion – usually falsely believing the truth would hurt – does not understand how some people lie as a way of life. Hitler surrounded himself with men who had this ability because he knew what he was planning was wrong and it would require an unlimited supply of lies to prevent any push-back.

2. Reprogramming the Human Mind

I believe that we are creations (programmed creations of a Creator) made in its image. We all have choice because programs have choice. If we choose one thing, something happens. If we choose another, something else happens. If-then. Cause and effect. It is all up to us individually and always has been. However, how can one make an informed choice without having access to all the information required for making that choice? The answer is, one cannot. That is why knowledge is so important and access to information is crucial to making informed choices. On the flip side of that, if people are interested in having us make choices that benefit their position, then they will control the information we have access to and limit it to only the information that favors that position. He who controls the information flow controls all because information creates knowledge and unlimited knowledge creates unlimited possibilities. If one wants to limit that knowledge to create a finite set of possibilities, then one must have the power to control the information so that it flows in certain directions only.

Hitler was certainly aware of this dynamic, as was Hermann Goering who testified at Nuremberg that the National Socialist German Workers Party, a/k/a the Nazi party was not interested in power for power's sake, but instead they needed power and governmental authority in order for them to carry out their agenda. They did not want to leave it to chance by putting it in the hands of free elections and Parliamentary majorities. They wanted to be able to rig the system so that they could carry out the task to which they considered themselves called.[24]

As Goering's testimony shows, Hitler and the men in his inner circle were power abusers in every sense of the word. They were not interested in using the power of their offices to ensure the rules of a democratic society were followed. They wanted to use their power to destroy democracy and ensure that Hitler's own personal world view was carried out as outlined in *Mein Kampf*.

As far as carrying out an agenda goes, the last thing a master illusionist wants is an individual with access to unlimited information. Hitler knew he had to control the information flow in order to limit the German citizen's knowledge as to his ultimate goals. It is the reason why propaganda played such a prominent role in his government. In terms of the role of human programming in making choices, propaganda is like garbage in-garbage out. It limits the processing capability of the human mind to output that is predictable and unchanging. That is why master illusionists love it so much. Outcomes are predictable and thereby can be better controlled.

Hitler and his gang needed the people to believe that the Nazi agenda was a good one so that they could achieve the outcome they wanted with as little resistance as possible. They knew well that people do not hold beliefs they think are wrong. They hold them because they believe them to be right, even if the rest of the world may see them as wrong. That is why in Nazi Germany, a Jewish, Russian or Czech mother could plead with an SS officer for the life of her child to no avail because in Nazi-controlled Germany, that soldier held the belief that Jews, Russians and Czechs were of no consequence.

> "One basic principle must be the absolute rule for the SS man. We must be honest, decent, loyal and comradely to members of our own blood and to nobody else. What happens to a Russian, to a Czech does not interest me in the slightest."[25]

It would have been pointless to try to reason with an SS soldier and convince him of the fact that on a biological level, there was no difference between him and a Russian, Jew or Czech because he had already been programmed to accept as fact that his German blood was superior. It made it very easy for him to put himself in a class that defined itself as pure German stock while putting everyone else in a "sub-human" class of beings that needed to be exterminated. This excerpt from the Nuremberg trial transcript shows how the programming made it very easy for the Nazi soldiers to exterminate Soviet soldiers and civilians en masse:

> "Evidence already in the record or shortly to be offered in case by our Soviet colleagues will prove that representatives of these Nazi conspirators did not hesitate to exterminate Soviet soldiers and civilians by scientific mass methods.

These inciting remarks by Fritzsche make him an accomplice in these crimes because his labeling of the Soviet peoples as members of a "subhuman world" seeking to "exterminate" the German people, and similar desperate talk, helped, by these propaganda diatribes, to fashion the psychological atmosphere of utter and complete unreason, and the hatred which instigated and made possible these atrocities in the East."[26]

It is very difficult for most, if not all people, to consciously do something wrong knowing it is wrong because it would mean they were bad people and no one wants to think of themselves as a bad person. That is where rationalizations, justifications and lies come in very handy. It allows us to consider ourselves good people in spite of actions that prove otherwise. The propaganda that filled the airwaves, newspapers and schoolbooks in Nazi Germany provided the Nazi soldiers and bureaucrats with all the rationalizations, justifications and lies they needed to continue thinking they were good in light of the actions they took that proved otherwise.

As for Hitler himself, he made people believe he was a good man doing God's work. At least that is the rationalization he used in all his passionate speeches to the public.[27] He did not view his hatred as a bad thing. Quite the contrary. Hitler viewed himself as a good man without having any empirical evidence to back up his belief. He was a nationalist who saw it as his mission to restore a mythic Germany that never existed in the first place to its rightful place as the ruling nation of Europe and eventually the world. In this mythic land, there was no place for any people who did not conform to the Nazi definition of what it meant to be a German. Unfortunately, the Jews, the handicapped, Christians, political dissidents, intellectuals, Slavs and all other people he perceived as undesirable all fell outside the definition. The holocaust, and really all the millions of lives that were lost during

WWII, was a good effect in Hitler's eyes because of his mind's belief that his cause was the work of God.

According to William Shirer, who wrote the following excerpt in *The Rise and Fall of the Third Reich*, Hitler had adopted the ideas pushed by the philosophers, Friedrich Nietzsche and Georg Wilhelm Friedrich Hegel, that a supreme leader is above the morals of ordinary men:

> "To judge morality properly, it must be replaced by two concepts borrowed from zoology: the taming of a beast and the breeding of a specific species. Such teachings, carried to their extremity by Nietzsche and applauded by a host of lesser Germans, seem to have exerted a strong appeal on Hitler. A genius with a mission was above the law; he could not be bound by "bourgeois" morals. Thus, when his time for action came, Hitler could justify the most ruthless and cold-blooded deeds, the suppression of personal freedom, the brutal practice of slave labor, the depravities of the concentration camp, the massacre of his own followers in 1934, the killing of war prisoners and the mass slaughter of the Jews."[28]

To me, it sounds like Shirer is describing the mind of a psychopath. Psychopaths are usually of average intelligence, but they feel superior to us mere mortals. We are restrained in what we will consider doing because of our sense of right and wrong. Psychopaths view that as weakness. They have no such restraints and they will lie, manipulate, undermine, harm and destroy anyone they perceive as a personal threat. According to Dr. Robert Hare, an expert in the field of psychopathy, a psychopath will not feel embarrassed or guilty when caught in a lie. They simply change the facts to suit the lie. They have become adept at rationalizing everything they do, so that even their most heinous acts seem reasonable in their minds. More often than not, their rationalizations convince them they are benefiting the organizations they work for and society as whole. They are emotionless people incapable of taking other people into consideration as they cause personal devastation all around them. [29]

A psychopathic personality is one that is adept at moving the bar of facts and reality into the realm of illusion. Hitler wasn't the only one moving the bar of reality in Nazi Germany with all his propaganda, false flag operations, manipulations and lies. The entire population was forced to move the bar of reality in their own minds if they wanted to survive financially, emotionally and physically. By moving the bar, they essentially became automatons of the party line with no independent thought of their own. Shirer describes this phenomenon so well in the following passage from *The Rise and Fall of the Third Reich*:

> "Often in a German home or office or sometimes in a casual conversation with a stranger in a restaurant, a beerhall, a café, I would meet with the most outlandish assertions from seemingly educated and intelligent. It was obvious that they were parroting some piece of nonsense they had heard on the radio or read in the newspapers. Sometimes one was tempted to say as much, but on such occasions one was met with such a stare of incredulity, sucha shock of silence, as if one had blasphemed the Almighty,that one realized how useless it was even to try to make contact with a mind which had become warped and for whom the facts of life were what Hitler and Goebbels, with their cynical disregard for truth, said they were."[30]

There is no brick wall quite as strong as a mind that has been made up and is determined not to change, for whatever reason. The individual human consciousness exists in the realm of information and ideas. It should always remain open so that it can change and evolve in accordance with what is true, rather than what someone else says is true. If not, it runs the risk of becoming a human automaton parroting the party line.

3. Propaganda

Propaganda serves to create illusory environments because the goal of propaganda is to get people to accept false assumptions. Illogical environments are often created by people who believe that the ends justify the means. When the end results you want to create go against an innate human spirit of decency, then the means must by default warp what is viewed as decent and good. It is no wonder the truth gets so lost in such environments where the people in power have the tools (means) for creating the environments (ends) they desire. Truth requires no such means. It just is. But as truth gets mired within the layers upon layers of false assumptions that the propaganda promotes, the ends the propaganda is promoting then get labeled as normal and truth tellers become the troublemakers, dissidents and whistle-blowers going against the norm of the newly created propagandized status quo. This is the process of evil. Evil is not like truth. Truth is black and white. Evil is the process of mixing reason with false premises to come up with the reasonable compromise of gray. Then as one layer of compromise gets built upon the next and the next and the next, it gets to the point where housing humans in camps and treating them with the respect bestowed upon cockroaches seems reasonable.

If we want to stay grounded in reality, we must always question our assumptions to ensure that they are factual and true. By doing so, we can be assured that any actions we take based upon those assumptions are right actions. Propaganda does the opposite. It convinces people to take actions based upon false information. In the case of Hitler, he didn't need to convince just one or two people that his views were right. He needed to convince an entire nation and the nations he conquered. To that end, propaganda was perfectly suited for addressing the broad masses of people who Hitler viewed as 'feeble intellects' who can only grasp the bare essentials without forgetting them.[31] Therefore, if propaganda was to work on them, he knew it had to appeal to their emotions rather than their reason. Additionally, it had to be limited to a few basic themes that are repeated over and over and over again. In his own words, "The greater the scope of the message that has to be presented, the more necessary it is for the propaganda to discover that plan of action which is psychologically the most efficient."[32]

Hitler wrote in *Mein Kampf* that it was necessary to avoid a high level of intellect in the propaganda. It was far more effective to appeal to baser human emotions like fear, anger, revenge, etc., if one wanted to sway the public sentiment:

> "When there is a question of bringing a whole nation within the circle of its influence, as happens in the case of war propaganda, then too much attention cannot be paid to the necessity of avoiding a high level [of intellect] … the more modest the scientific tenor of this propaganda and the more it is addressed exclusively to the public sentiment, the more decisive will be its success."[33]

Hitler killed the intellectuals in all the countries he overtook because it was hard to get them to believe the propaganda when they were trained in dealing with facts:

> "The planned execution of intelligentsia and other Russian leaders was, for example, but a part of   the actual operation of the program to destroy the Soviet Union politically and make impossible its early resurrection as a European power."[34]

In addition to killing off the intellectuals, Hitler also eradicated any opposition journalists who gave differing views concerning the Nazi agenda. When August Fritzsche, a senior official who served as the Director of the Reich Ministry of Public Enlightenment and Propaganda, undertook the task of bringing all news agencies in Germany under Fascist control, he learned that his former occupation as an opposition journalist no longer existed because opposition journalism has been forced out of existence. Having realized this, Fritzche had a decision to make. He could either use his position to stand up for freedom of the press or he could retain his cushy job as a propagandist with a fancy title serving the Nazi agenda. He chose the latter and became the preeminent German broadcaster of his time, doing his part to present "a more popular and entertaining side of the Nazi regime."[35]

As a popular propagandist for the Nazi machine, Fritzsche played a huge role in swaying public opinion. That is why the prosecutors at the Nuremberg trials held the propagandists to be just as culpable as the chief planners of the conspiracy. Without them, most ordinary German citizens would never have participated in the atrocities or turned the other way as their neighbors were taken away.

3a. Role of Mass Media in Propaganda

Previous to Hitler's rise to power and his establishment of the Reich in Germany, the country was set up somewhat similarly to the Republic of the United States of America. Each German state was a sovereign territory under the German Republic's Weimar Constitution and it was governed by that state's laws in cases where there was no governing federal law. After the passage of the Enabling Act, those same states, provinces and municipalities lost their sovereignty. The physical state boundaries became administrative-technical boundaries and the states themselves were considered administrative organs of the central government.[36] As administrative organs of the central government, they were governed by the laws of the Reich and were responsible for upholding those laws.

However, the use of centralization was not limited to the government in Hitler's Germany. It extended to all facets of society-even to mass media. Hitler would claim there was freedom of the press, but he knew better. The structure in place for moderating the press limited it to one voice only when it came to the messaging that the German population received. In his role as Reich Minister of Propaganda, Josef Goebbels dictated what the German people saw and heard and he did it through the German Press Division.

The German Press Division was the instrument for subordinating the entire German press to the political aims of the government. With more than 2,300 newspapers subject to its control, along with the publications of all official governmental agencies, the German Press Division worked something like this. Each day, the head of the German Press Division was given directives from Goebbels and other ministries of the Reich. The directives were then communicated to the representatives of all German newspapers through the use of a statement called the "Daily Parole of the Reich Press Chief" and they were all expected to follow those directives. The publications of all official agencies were also similarly directed and coordinated through the German Press Division. In this way, the entire German Press was made subordinate to the government's political agenda.[37]

The prosecutors at Nuremberg explained how the German Press Division was an important psychological tool of the Nazi conspirators for conforming the minds of the population to accepting war against other nations:

"These functions [the functions of the German Press Division] show the important and unique position of the German Press Division as an instrument of the Nazi conspirators, not only in the minds and the psychology of Germans through the German Press Division and through the radio, but also as an instrument of foreign policy and psychological warfare against other nations."[38]

As the above passage shows, the centralization of control over information became especially useful for disseminating war propaganda. The pre-invasion headlines and newspaper articles regarding Yugoslavia is a prime example of the Nazi conspirators' use of the press to defame, lie and threaten another nation in order to weaken it, as illustrated in the following excerpt:

"The German Press emphasised by headlines and leading articles the following topics: (1) the planned persecution of Germans in Yugoslavia, including the burning down of German villages by Serbian soldiers; the confining of Germans in concentration camps, and also the physical mishandling of German-speaking persons; (2) the arming of Serbian bandits by the Serbian Government; (3) the incitement of Yugoslavia by the plutocrats against Germany; (4) the increasing anti-Serbian feeling in Croatia; (5) the chaotic economic and social conditions in Yugoslavia."[39]

None of the headlines and articles about Yugoslavia were true, but they were very effective in rallying support for the invasion. In the case of the Soviet Union, the German Press Division went even further. Joachim von Ribbentrop, foreign minister under the Nazi regime asked the German Press Division to present the invasion of the Soviet Union as a war that was forced upon Germany as a defensive measure because Germany was facing an imminent attack by the Soviet Union.[40] Again none of it was true, but that is par for the course in illusory environments where truth and reality must be destroyed in order to make way for the master illusionists to create their own reality.

Central to the art of propaganda is the ability to get people to accept re-definitions of words and people. If you can change meanings of words so that they become more amenable to your agenda, what is commonly called political correctness in our present day and age, then the people will act in accordance with those new meanings.

One of the most outrageous re-definitions Hitler made was to categorize the invasion of Austria as a liberation rather than an unwanted invasion of a sovereign country. In a speech he made to the Austrian people shortly after occupation of their country, he told them,

> "Certain foreign newspapers have said that we fell on Austria with brutal methods. I can only say: even in death they cannot stop lying. I have in the course of my political struggle won much love from my people, but when I crossed the former frontier [into Austria] there met me such a stream of love as I have never experienced. Not as tyrants have we come, but as liberators."[41]

Changing the word 'tyrant' to 'liberator' was a very effective propaganda technique for obtaining support for Hitler's invasion agenda of Austria and as can be attested to, it has stood the test of time very well for those willing to use the same technique [lie] to justify their own war agendas.

4. Using Rationalizations, Justifications and Blame to Justify Our Irrational Thinking and Absolve Ourselves of Guilt

Hitler used a distorted interpretation of the philosophies of Nietzche and Hegel to justify his belief that he was above the law and not subject to the bourgeois morality that bound lesser men. In fact, it is through this justification that he made himself supreme leader of

Germany and was able to institute policies that justified the suppression of freedom, the limitation of rights and all the crimes against humanity his regime committed.[42]

When corrupted minds like Hitler's are in control of a community of people, whether it be a home, business, government or world organization, the result is the same. The 'lesser' people in their minds, who do have a sense of morality and goodness, begin to feel like up is down, down is up, right is wrong and wrong is right. A big factor in creating those feelings on their part is that the corrupted 'masters' in charge have used thought maneuvers like rationalizations, justification, lies and scapegoating to make behavior they consciously know is wrong into seemingly right behavior..

Perhaps the most horrific and hideous rationalization the regime's leadership ever used was what they labeled 'the final solution' because this positive sounding phrase (dare I say politically correct use of the word 'solution') was used to justify the torture and killing of their innocent fellow human beings. Adolf Eichmann was one of the creators of this rationalization. Years later, when he was finally arrested for the crimes he committed under the umbrella that he was solving a problem, one of the arresting officers noticed how concerned he was about his own wife and children and worried about how they would get on once he was gone. Astonished at Eichmann's lack of guilt or remorse for the millions of mothers and children he had a hand in killing, the officer asked him how he could have murdered so many families while having so much empathy and concern for his own. His answer was that he wanted to find a satisfactory solution to *their* problem and that he just wanted to get on in life by doing what everyone else was doing.[43]

These kinds of amoral justifications were used by all the Nazi leadership to act illegally and immorally. Another example can be found in the formation of an organization called the Einsatzstab Reichsleiter Rosenberg (ERR). The ERR was originally established for the purpose of collecting and suppressing undesirable political media but it quickly devolved into an agency that stole the private art collections of Jews across Europe.[44] They justified the thievery by saying it is a well-established principle of international law during times of war that reprisals can be taken against an enemy by using the same concepts and procedures as propagated by that enemy. Thus, the ERR justified its theft of Jewish property by saying that the Talmud and ancient Jewish laws consider all non-Jews as no better than cattle and therefore without the rights accorded to man. I am not familiar with the Talmud and what it says or the context of this passage. However, the Nazi interpretation provided them with justification for their theft. They reasoned that if the Jews themselves were allowed to view non-Jews as no better than cattle under the Talmud, then it was fine for the non-Jew Nazi to view the Jews in a similar manner. It was a tit for tat rationalization where two wrongs do make a right. When the Belgian, Dutch and French protested the actions of the ERR under international law, their protestations fell on deaf ears because in the minds of the Nazi thieves, the justification had already given them permission to act as they did.[45]

All these same kinds of justifications and rationalization were used to plunder the land and steal the homes and resources of the peoples across eastern Europe.[46] Hitler and the Nazi regime needed rationalizations, justifications and lies for its very existence. As I said earlier, no one wants to think of themselves as a bad person and rationalizations give them the wiggle room for creating a gray area where they can view themselves as good people. Rationalizations give people the leeway to commit the most horrible acts against their fellow human beings, while allowing them to still feel good about themselves.

They provide the perfect means for turning the non-good into the good.

As I discuss later in the book, rationalizations and justifications are what I believe Jesus was referring to when he accused some Pharisees of committing sin that cannot be forgiven because they make a person believe that wrong thinking is right thinking and thereby prevents that person from ever taking any corrective action in changing that thinking.

4a. *"In the Interest of National Security" Rationalization (lie)*

The S.S. (Secret State Police) was originally formed to spy on members of the Social Democratic Party who were labeled radical because they opposed the Nazi State. Goering testified at his trial that he eventually had all the Social Democrats arrested and put in concentration camps in the interest of national security. As the following passage from the Nuremberg trial transcript states, the concentration camps were not built for the Jews. They were originally built to house the Communists put in protective custody as a means of preventing them from committing any hostile acts against the State, regardless of any proof they had that those arrested were involved in traitorous acts or whether one could expect such acts from them in the future.

> "We had to deal ruthlessly with these enemies of the State. It should not be forgotten that at the moment of our seizure of power, over 6,000,000 people officially voted for Communism and about 8,000,000 for Marxism in the Reichstag elections in March. Thus the Concentration Camps were created, to which we had to send first, thousands of functionaries of the Communist and Social Democratic parties."[47]

Soon after, however, concentration camps were used to house anyone who would "endanger the security of the people and the State through their attitude."[48]

Putting someone in protective custody in a concentration camp was a preventive measure done in the interest of national security. Protective custody itself was a rationalization used to hold people indefinitely without charge or due process. According to Wikipedia, protective custody is a type of imprisonment or care to protect a person from harm, either from outside sources or other prisoners. The Nazi regime turned the process on its ear by saying that Communists and other undesirables in the eyes of the State who had opinions that differed from those of the party line were a danger to the State itself and needed to be locked away. It ensnared thousands in its net whether they were actually guilty of anything or not.[49] Wilhelm Keitel, field marshal and head of the German Armed Forces High Command during World War II, decided to forego protective custody altogether and ordered that any individual(s) suspected of being a terrorist, as defined by the State as a dissenter of the State's policies, be killed. It was a means of destroying the resistance movements and subduing the populations in the countries Hitler invaded.[50]

5. Devaluation of the Individual Human Being (sub-human)

Recent studies into the phenomenon of bullying and workplace mobbing find that targets of bullying/mobbing are dehumanized so that the abusers can justify the severe mistreatment of their victims. When the recipient of the abuse is not seen as an equal human being, it is more easy to denigrate, belittle and humiliate them. The target thereby becomes a mere object in the eyes of the abuser not deserving of treatment normally afforded a fellow human being.[51]

It never occurred to me before doing the research for this book that the word 'extermination', which I had heard used countless times for the killing of Jews in Nazi Germany, is not a word we normally use for the killing of human beings. It is a word we use for the killing of cockroaches and other insects. However, it was the word used in Nazi Germany because that is the level the Jews were put on in Nazi Germany. They didn't even bother trying to find a politically correct word for extermination in reference to the Jews gassed to death in concentration camps. They didn't have to because they looked at Jews as sub-humans on the level of cockroaches. Cockroaches are not killed or murdered. They are exterminated.

The truth is that we would never have had to lose so many lives and endure so much suffering as that era of our history wrought if Hitler had not used and abused the power of his position to create the powerful propaganda machine that got other people to adopt the same frame of mind he had. The propaganda machine worked very effectively in helping to dehumanize the Jews by pounding into the consciousness of the German population that the Jews were the cause of all the country's economic troubles after WWII. In his testimony at the Nuremberg trials, Erich von dem Bach-Zelewski, Police Leader in Central Russia during Hitler's campaign against the Soviet Union, stated that the extermination of thirty million Slavs was "a natural result of a doctrine that was preached to the effect that the Slav race is an inferior race, and Jews not even human at all."[52]

Himmler also pushed the ideas that Hitler put forth in *Mein Kampf* that certain groups of individuals were sub-human.. He lumped the Bolshevists (Communists) together with the Jews and classified both groups as an internal sub-human threat to Germany:

"We shall unremittingly fulfil our task, the guaranty of the security of Germany from the interior, just as theWehrmacht guarantees the safety of the honour, the greatness, and the peace of the Reich from the exterior. <u>We take care that never again in Germany, the heart of Europe, will the Jewish-Bolshevistic revolution of subhumans be able to be kindled either from within or through emissaries from without.</u> Without pity we shall be a merciless sword of justice for all those forces whose existence and activity we know, on the day of the slightest attempt, may it be today, may it be in decades or may it be in centuries."[53]

People did not become convinced that their Jewish neighbors, colleagues and friends were sub-human overnight. It was a gradual process that began with labels like troublemaker, dissident and non-team player that serve to separate a specific person or group out from the crowd. This isolation and exclusion then allows them to be targeted for escalated forms of abuse where they can be picked off one-by-one by bystanders and enablers who want to stay safe and in the good graces of the leader.

It would not have served the self-interests of anyone working for the judicial system, penal system or military in Hitler's Germany to question the assumption that their blood was superior to that of the people being labeled sub-human. It was their job to subjugate and/or kill these sub-humans. It would have been career suicide, or more likely death, to point out the obvious.

The purpose of the propaganda was to protect their minds while they were subjugating and killing their fellow human beings. How could they continue to think of themselves as good, decent and honest people if they were to accept the fact they were killing people who were no different from their own mothers, fathers, sisters, children and brothers? The killing business requires the propaganda that portrays people just like ourselves as enemies, villains, troublemakers, dissidents and sub-human terrorists out to destroy our way of life.

Leaders, managers, politicians, and authoritarians of all stripes and colors who are willing to abuse their power in this way are essentially denying the reality that all human beings are equal at the level of energy. The Bible tells us as much in Genesis when it says all humans are created in the image of God and Science has empirically proven it in its study of the laws of nature and energy. That could be why the leading members of Hitler's National Socialist Democratic Party hated both Christians and Jews and preferred Occultism over Science.

When the agendas of the people holding positions of power are contrary to the truth, it turns our external environments upside-down and makes it extremely difficult to make logical and right decisions without suffering negative consequences. As long as the SS soldier held the false assumption that his elite blood was superior, he could follow orders that required him to commit crimes against humanity. If he were ever to question the assumption and come to the conclusion that it was in fact false, it could lead to some very serious consequences on a spiritual level, not to mention a physical level.

6. The Process Used for the Targeting and Mobbing of Human Beings

Hitler was very interested in creating a Nazi-ruled new order in all the countries he conquered. In this new order, the resources of those countries would be exploited for Nazi profit and the people enslaved or exterminated; particularly the intelligentsia of those countries. To Hitler and his leadership corps, the people themselves had no value except to the extent that they could be used as work slaves. As each country was taken over, their cultures were to be permanently eradicated along with all education, so that they could be re-educated (indoctrinated) into accepting a fascist way of life in keeping with the beliefs of their Nazi overlords.

Heinrich Himmler, in his role as chief of the S.S. and the entire police apparatus of the Third Reich, wrote in a secret memo to members of the S.S. "whether nations live in prosperity or starve to death like cattle interests me only in so far as we need them as slaves to our Kultur; otherwise it is of no interest to me. Whether 10,000 Russian females fall down from exhaustion while digging an antitank ditch interests me only in so far as the antitank ditch for Germany is finished.[54]

A very methodical process was instituted to target and eliminate entire groups of people who had no place in the new order that Hitler envisioned. A particularly cruel and vicious form of targeting was conducted against the Jews in order to get their neighbors, colleagues and friends to turn against them. However, some variation of targeting was used against all groups who were identified for slave labor and/or elimination.

Not a lot of research has been done into the human targeting process known as 'mobbing' and that is quite surprising given that this phenomenon of human targeting was used so extensively in Nazi Germany, as well as in the Communist nations that Hitler learned it from. It has been around since at least the time of King David and Saul, continuing into the first millennium when it was employed by the Pharisees against Jesus and most certainly much longer than that. It is behavior arising out of an animal consciousness, so it probably dates all the way back to when people inhabited caves. In fact, I have used the word 'illusion' to describe what the Bible calls evil, but really, it is simply the application of an animal consciousness to a human consciousness that has evolved way beyond its animal origins. It is a de-evolutionary process that minds like Hitler use to create a state of stasis in a human species that is created to eternally change, grow and evolve. By creating external structures and rigging the systems within those structures, an animalistic human consciousness is able to put limits on the ever-expanding human minds it seeks to control.

Professor Kenneth Westhues has conducted research on mobbing. Although his research was limited to the area of academia, I think his definition of the practice is the best I have come across yet in all my own research on the subject. Westhues defines mobbing as "an impassioned, collective campaign to exclude, punish, and humiliate a targeted worker. Initiated most often by a person in a position of power or influence, mobbing is a desperate urge to crush and eliminate the target. The urge travels through the workplace [or in the case of Hitler and the N.S.D.A.P., through a country and the countries they invaded] like a virus, infecting one person after another. The target comes to be viewed as absolutely abhorrent, with no redeeming qualities, outside the circle of acceptance and respectability, deserving only of contempt. As the campaign proceeds, a steadily larger range of ploys and communications comes to be seen as legitimate."[55]

Various experiments have proven it to be the case that good and decent people can easily become cruel and sadistic within certain organizational settings where an authoritarian figure has "made it clear that certain individuals are undesirable, may be mistreated, shunned, and even falsely accused of misconduct and crimes."[56]

In his seminal work on the subject, Dr. Heinz Leymann identified manipulation as the main characteristic of a mobbing and identified the five key manipulations used in a mobbing as follows: (1) the target's good reputation is destroyed with rumors, slander and lies; (2) communications with the targeted individual become hostile and all attempts by the individual to be heard are blocked or denied; (3) the targeted individual is isolated from his colleagues; (4) the ability of the targeted individual to do his work is made impossible by giving him no work or giving him meaningless tasks to do; and (5) violence or threats of violence are directed against the targeted individual. It is no wonder why Leymann referred to mobbing as psychic terror.[57] These manipulations leave the target isolated and alone with no help to be had, no means for making a living and the threat of incarceration and/or physical harm always looming.

In Nazi Germany, after the Jews were stripped of all their possessions with no means of escape once they were packed like sardines into rail cars that transported them to the camps. They were even refused help from the people who were tasked with helping them. One witness at Nuremberg stated, "At the station of Rheims water was refused us by the German Red Cross. We were dying of thirst. In Breslau the prisoners again begged nurses of the German Red Cross to give us a little water. They refused and remained unmoved by our appeals."[58]

Unfortunately, that is what happens in corrupt environments. Even the people whose job it is to help you will turn their backs on you because they have been just as propagandized and immobilized by fear as the rest of the population.

Although the research I have found on the topic of mobbing is mainly limited to the workplace, my research on Hitler and Nazi Germany has shown me that the targeting process is certainly not limited to the workplace. Given that we are now a global community of people through the Internet and technology, it can be expanded far out from the workplace to include communities of people contained in countries and even the world.

It is estimated that between two and five percent of adults are mobbed at some point during their work lives and the other 95 percent are involved in the mobbing as perpetrators, enablers and bystanders. One of the reasons cited by Westhues as to why so little research has been performed on a practice that causes 12% of its intended targets to commit suicide is because the 95% of people involved in the mobbing mostly deny or gloss over their own roles in the destruction of the target's life.

The hierarchical structure of many workplaces could explain why the percentage of participants in a mobbing is as high as 95% and so very few people, if any, are willing to come to a target's aid. The bystanders and enablers of a mobbing will side with the ringleader for fear that if they don't, they themselves will become the next target. It is really no wonder why Hitler chose the structure for ruling Germany and the countries he took over.

As the statistics show, so much of the ugliness of the human mind arises from the unnatural and man-made hierarchies that designate some human beings as more valuable than other human beings. Why do we continue to hand out these false titles? I think the imbalance in power these titles create makes bullying and mob-like behavior the corrosive problem it is in our societies at large and in our workplaces in particular. With management almost always taking up arms with the power abusing colleague and fellow employees on the target's row of the hierarchy abandoning the target out of fear of becoming targets themselves, the victims of mobbings are unfortunately left on their own most of the time. It is this sense of exclusion, isolation, abandonment and betrayal by people the target has come to like and respect that leads to the helplessness and frustration so many targets and whistle blowers feel.

6a. Isolation and Exclusion (banishment)

Hitler was an expert in the five key manipulations used in a mobbing that were identified by Heinz Leymann in the 1990's. Isolation of the target from his colleagues was one of them and as Hitler proved, isolation becomes a key component in the mobbing ritual.

The divide and conquer strategy inherent in a mobbing works in separating those people willing to speak up against the abuse from the ones who are fearful and willing to participate out of that fear. Whistle blowers are known as 'troublemakers' in corrupt work environments and are labeled as such for purposes of targeting. When it is a government doing the targeting, the preferred label is 'dissidents.' Much like Hitler used terror techniques to harass and silence the people he viewed as dissidents and troublemakers, many employers likewise use abusive behaviors like rumor mongering, intimidation, humiliation, innuendo and other forms of character assassination to isolate targets and deem them as undesirable and dangerous to the rest of the organization. As the mob grows, it feeds off the energy created when the targeted person begins to break down and act crazy as they perceive it. It gives them someone to blame (a scapegoat) and makes them feel righteous in their cause because the break down indicates guilt in their eyes. That is how the tables of morality get turned upside-down and what is considered right (helping the targeted person) becomes wrong. It is a slimy, dirty, disgusting technique for getting rid of someone you don't like while keeping your own hands clean.

Hitler targeted people he did not like and he used the techniques of mobbing to cancel them from society. The holocaust did not happen overnight. It was a methodical process where every detail was thoroughly planned out. The steps of the process that included exclusion, isolation, degradation, humiliation and character assassination eventually led to physical elimination of entire groups of people.

Beginning with his writing of *Mein Kampf*, Hitler created the perception in the minds of the population that Jews were not German. He then used this justification to pass laws denying them access to public services, universities and the professions. In 1933, he asked for a boycott of Jewish shops and in 1935, the Nuremberg laws were enacted which deprived Jews of citizenship, confining them to the status of subjects. Also, it was these laws that allowed the Jews to be segregated into ghettos and made into forced laborers. All their property was confiscated, they were denied access to schools. By 1936, the year Germany hosted the Olympics, nearly half the Jewish population was unable to make a living having been denied private and public employment.[59]

> All these laws and policies served to isolate the Jews from German society and exclude them from getting an education and obtaining employment. It was this process of isolation and exclusion that allowed the Nazis to easily find the Jews and capture them without resistance because by then, they lacked the material, physical and intellectual resources that would have enabled them to launch a counter attack against their persecutors.[60]

6b. Humiliation and Degradation

Another key manipulation used in a mobbing is the process of humiliating and degrading the target so that they are not seen as valuable and productive members of the group. A German citizen in Nazi Germany was bombarded with signs, newspaper articles, pamphlets and propaganda on all fronts, the purpose of which was to humiliate their Jewish neighbors and colleagues:

> "In many a town the Jew found it difficult if not impossible to purchase food. Over the doors of the grocery and butcher shops, the bakeries and the

dairies, were signs, "Jews Not Admitted." In many communities Jews could not procure milk even for their young children. Pharmacies would not sell them drugs or medicine. Hotels would not give them a night's lodging. And always, wherever they went, were the taunting signs "Jews Strictly Forbidden in This Town" or "Jews Enter This Place at Their Own Risk." Sharp Curve! Jews 75 Miles an Hour!"* Such was the plight of the Jews at about the time the Festival of the Olympics was held in Germany. It was but the beginning of a road that would soon lead to their extinction by massacre."[61]

Josef Goebbels' Propaganda Ministry went into full gear to debase the Jews. The ministry conducted a full-fledged campaign to break the Jews in order to clear the way for their extermination. From the leadership on down to the person on the street, nothing that was said or done was beyond the pale in this campaign. Once in the concentration camps, the living conditions assured their death:

Through inadequate feeding, bad sanitation, cruelty of the guards, severity of discipline, strain of work out of proportion to the strength of the prisoner, and haphazard medical service. Moreover, you already know that many did not die a natural death, but were put to death by injections, gas chambers or inoculations of fatal diseases. However, more speedy extermination was often the case and was brought about by ill treatment: communal ice-cold showers in winter in the open air, prisoners left naked in the snow, cudgeling [getting beaten with a club], attacks by dogs and hanging by the wrists."[62]

Even before entering the camps, many people died in the trains that brought them to the camps. They were oftentimes kept completely unclothed to not only humiliate them, but to also prevent them from escaping. In fact, many traveled from France to Germany completely naked in the Nazi efforts to completely degrade and demoralize them.[63]

The perpetrators of a mobbing purposely go after their target's spirit with acts of humiliation and degradation in order to make them feel a sense of worthlessness about themselves and make everyone else think the target is the cause of the problems and not the power abuser or abusers who initiated the conflict. Since people want to side with the winner, they join in the campaign of degradation and destruction.

6c. Provide No Means for Resolution or Escape (destruction of target is aim)

As with all mobbings, there comes a point where there is no means for salvation or escape. A 1943 decree marked that point for the Jews in Germany and the occupied countries, whereby the court system became unavailable to them. The police and SS became the sole arbiters of punishment and death.[64]

7. Projection

As becomes obvious when one reads *Mein Kampf*, Hitler over and over again makes statements as if they are proven facts. The method he uses for doing this is called projection. With projection, a person either consciously or subconsciously attributes their own personal characteristics onto someone else. I say subconsciously because in many cases, the person may not be aware that they are projecting. That is particularly true in the case of someone who has never performed any kind of self-examination to determine their belief system, strengths, weaknesses, values, etc.

Hitler's favorite target of projection was the Jews. What follows are just two of many examples littered throughout *Mein Kampf.* Hitler wrote that throughout history the Jews have risen to power through obfuscation and deceit, but once in power, they throw off all the veils and reveal themselves not as a Jew of the people, but as a tyrant. Then, in the course of a few years they exterminate all those who represent the national intelligence. And by thus depriving the peoples of their natural intellectual leaders he fits them for their fate as slaves under a lasting despotism.[65]

I do not know what Jews Hitler was talking about when he wrote that they used the tactics of tyrants to rise to power and then destroy all the intellectuals who threatened to dispose. What I do know is that is exactly what Hitler did in Germany and Poland when he took those countries over. One of his first orders of business was to kill off all the intelligentsia:

> "The Fuhrer stressed once more that there should be one master only for the Poles -- the German: two masters, side by side, cannot and must not exist; therefore, all representatives of the Polish intelligentsia are to be exterminated. This sounds cruel, but such is the law of life."[66]

Hitler also said that, if given the chance, the Jews would take control of the press in order to take over and control the state. They would then use the press to sabotage the nation's cultural values and destroy its national independence and the autonomy of its economic system. As we all know, it was Hitler, along with Josef Goebbels, who controlled the press in their efforts to obtain control over the state and they did it in exactly that same way - by sabotaging Germany's cultural values and destroying its national independence and the autonomy of its economic system by centralizing it under the state.

But it wasn't only the Jews who were the objects of Hitler's projection. He projected onto all his perceived enemies his own behaviors and shortcomings. It was a way for him to deflect the masses into thinking he was a good guy while making the Jews and Social Democrats the bad guys who were seeking to obtain control over their nation. It was never him. It was always them. In reality, it was him and only him, but he could not have anyone knowing that until his power was fully consolidated and it was too late for anyone to do anything about it.

8. Upside-Down View of Strength and Weakness

Hitler was an artist with a lot of passion in him. Each time he failed, he channeled that passion into a new pursuit. He didn't get into Art School, so he conformed his passion by convincing himself that Architecture School would be a better fit for him. Then when he didn't get into Architecture School, the job of bureaucrat that his father originally pushed him toward became his new driving force.[67]

However, as passionate and forceful a speaker as he was, Hitler may have found himself out of his element in his role as leader of a nation. As many power abusers do when lacking in confidence for the new roles they may find themselves in, Hitler compensated by putting on a show of force as a means of showing people how he was 'a man of action.' In his trial testimony at Nuremberg, Adolf von Steengracht, Secretary of State of the Reich Foreign Office from May 1943, provided some very valuable insights into Hitler's character when he said the following:

> "In the course of my activities, covering almost two years, I can now recall almost no case in which he agreed to one of our suggestions. On the contrary, it was always to be feared that through some objection of a personal nature he wouldbe led to take forceful action in an opposite direction. The basic trait of his character was probably lack of confidence, and this bore unprecedented fruit. Thus, experts and decent people who tried to influence Hitler to their way of thinking were engaged, in my opinion, in an altogether vain task. On the other hand, irresponsible people who incited him to take violent measures or to voice his suspicions, unfortunately

found him extremely accessible. These men were then termed "strong," whereas the behaviour of anyone who was even half-way towards normal was called "weak" or "defeatist;" through a sensible opinion voiced only once, the influence of that man could be forever destroyed."[68]

According to this passage, Hitler did not listen to the advice of decent and logical people because he considered them weak. The ones who caught his ear were those who encouraged him to take violent measures. They were the ones he considered strong. The more Hitler's inner circle conveyed views contradictory to basic feelings of humanity, the more Hitler liked them.[69]

Adolf von Steengracht further testified that Hitler detested the Foreign Office and told them that diplomacy is treason and that treaties are childish and are only to be followed when they work to one's advantage. Hitler's thinking turned everything upside-down, which is why von Steengracht said anyone who was even halfway normal in Hitler's circle was deemed weak and thereby forever destroyed. By eliminating all the decent people from his administration, Hitler effectively doomed Germany and the world because there were no longer any good men left in his government to steer Hitler into a different course of action from the destructive one he was hell bent on taking.[70]

Hitler's love of violence did not escape the notice of the prosecutors at Nuremberg. In making their case, the prosecutors frequently quoted passages from *Mein Kampf* that illustrate Hitler's belief that mankind's struggle for existence requires force and that all doctrines encouraging peaceable solutions to international problems represent weakness in any nation that adopts them. In fact, they describe it as the underlying message of the entire book.[71]

Hitler had an upside-down view of human strength and

weakness because he held an animalistic view of the world; seeing it as a jungle where only the fittest survive and the strongest rule. He believed it was through a process of natural selection that allowed the best of the human species to survive. However, his was a perverted interpretation of Darwin's theory of natural selection. Darwin believed that the strongest of the human species survived generation after generation because they had the ability to adapt to changing environments. In Hitler's view, it was not a matter of adaptability but rather a matter of who the best destroyer is. This belief led to what can only be described as his worship of the Aryan race, believing that the race had survived and accomplished so much because it was willing to trample over others in its fight for supremacy.[72]

This philosophy that defines 'strong' in animal terms begs the question... what does it mean to be strong? In my opinion, only a weak human being believes that accomplishment comes from physically trampling the rights of others. That is the easy way. It takes courage and intelligence to convince others to work with you to derive solutions that benefit the interests of all parties involved.

Applying the law of the jungle to conscious and eternally evolving human minds has a devolving effect on evolution. And Hitler is a prime example. He tossed the world into a global war where millions of innocent men, women and children died, cultural artifacts impossible to replace were destroyed, cities were left in ruins, millions were displaced, millions more were left psychologically damaged and for what? So that the deluded dreams of a man who was psychologically damaged himself could be achieved? What kind of motivation is that for a country of rational men and women?

True strength does not lie in destruction. Destruction is easy. Evolution is hard because it involves growth in every sense of the word. True strength is the ability to truthfully analyze yourself, your motivations and your reasons for doing what you do, so that you can eliminate any false assumptions underpinning your world view and belief systems. Anyone who does this is incapable of rationalizing any actions not based on what is true.

If Hitler had performed a truthful exercise of weeding out false thought forms from his mind, he would have realized that what is true is that the Aryans were no different from the Jews or anyone else in that they came into this world the same way and go out the same. He accomplished nothing by trampling over others except what all bullies and power abusers accomplish: the illusory win in an illusory game of their own making. The physical jungle for human beings does not exist and to pretend it does in order to justify one's abusive actions is the marker of a very weak person incapable of dealing with truth and reality.

Unfortunately, thoughts largely arising out of our collective survival consciousness of eat or be eaten has created a system (matrix if you will) that requires us to live much of our time with a mind stuck in the gray area of illusion and false assumptions for purposes of keeping our personal welfare and the welfare of our families intact. However, it might be well to keep in mind that although maintaining the false mindset required for survival may keep a roof over your head and food on the table, it does come with a heavy cost. Lack of logic and truth is the natural habitat for a mind consumed with survival. At some point in your life, you will inevitably clash with people whose own survival requires them to take actions in conflict with your survival. That is the time when you will have to make some very difficult decisions that may or may not result in harm to yourself and/or others.

I began this section of the book with an illustration of how Hitler was able to conform his thinking so that each failure in his life became a victory of sorts in his mind. I will now end it with William Shirer's depiction of an incident he read about after the war which illustrates the strong effect the illusion can have on our minds if we refuse to deal with truth in all our feelings, thoughts and actions. After the war, a journalist wrote about visiting a camp where they were confining SS prisoners-of-war. One of prisoners did not understand why he was there and asked the correspondent why he was being charged as a war criminal if all he had done was perform his duties as a soldier. This SS soldier had absolutely no idea why he was being held or what he did wrong because he had just followed the orders of his superiors. The SS in Nazi Germany was in charge of running the concentration camps and was notorious for brutalizing and murdering individuals in territories occupied by Germany. That is the organization and work that this soldier signed up for and when held to account for the atrocities he committed in his line of work, all he had was the time-honored defense that he was just doing what he was told.

9. Secrecy - to hide true intentions

We have a lot to learn from Hitler and his regime, but we have mistakenly chosen to hide from the process of learning from them by banning the sale of *Mein Kampf* in many jurisdictions and not giving academia the leeway to teach about the Nazi era in a way that exposes the thinking of the Nazi mind so that we can avoid it in our own minds. This lack of knowledge has legitimized many actions that mirror the Nazi regime. Secrecy and the protection of national secrets in the interest of national security have become mainstream, while at the same time we persecute and prosecute people who act in favor of truth by bringing those secrets out into the light.

It is important to note that while it was actually happening, very little was known of all the treachery and maneuvering taking place behind the scenes in the Third Reich. The public had to wait until the secret documents recorded at these secret meeting were confiscated by the Allies and the facts were revealed at the Nuremberg trials.[73]

It was revealed during the trials that one such meeting took place at Hitler's headquarters on July 16, 1941.[74] This particular meeting was very revealing in that it was attended by some of the key players and it laid out their plans regarding the war in the East. The transcript of the meeting very clearly shows how the Nazi conspirators planned on deceiving the entire world by pretending they would follow one course of action, as they actually followed a different one. Their lies in saying one thing and doing another was a key strategy in their efforts to Germanise the conquered areas of the Soviet Union and eventually, the entire world. In pursuing their deceptive strategy, they presented themselves as 'liberators'. They never intended to leave the countries they invaded, but they had to keep that a secret so that no one was able to recognize their intent to make the countries final settlements. After all, liberators sounds so much better than invaders.[75] It serves its purpose so well in fooling the bystanders and enablers of this world that you are doing something noble while quite the opposite is true.

The meeting transcript conclusively showed that Hitler and his inner circle were each acting with a consciousness of knowing their actions were wrong. All their defenses of saying they were just following orders or that if they had known the end goal they would never have done what they did, crumble under the light of facts. Even if some the generals and soldiers situated lower on the pyramid were not privy to information regarding the long-term goals, due to compartmentalization and the process of giving out information on a need-to-know basis, the inner circle certainly knew that what they were doing was in conflict with the principles of international law. Yet they did it anyway because it served them. If the facts were otherwise, they would not have needed all the secrecy and deception.

The Nuremberg trials were flawed in many respects and allowed for many of the participants in the Nazi atrocities to get off with light sentences or even escape punishment entirely. However, what the trials did do well was to reveal all the plotting and machinations that went on secretly, behind closed doors; hidden from the eyes of journalists and the German general public, which the Nazi leadership was so quick to say they were serving.

Most of the cabinet meetings and conferences held by Hitler and his inner circle were held in the strictest secrecy and the discussions they had within these meetings were classified as state secrets. One of these state secrets was what the Nazi conspirators called *the Final Solution*. After lengthy discussions, it was decided that the Jewish question would be solved by eliminating Jews from the German economy and transferring all Jewish assets and property to Aryan hands with some compensation in the form of bonds from which Jews could use the interest but not the capital. As part of the so-called solution, Jews were banned from schools, resorts, beaches, public parks, etc. Ultimately, they were interned in camps where they would be constricted into forced labor or killed.[76]

In his testimony at Nuremberg, Rudolf Hoess, Commandant of Auschwitz, described how he was summoned to Berlin in 1941, where he was told by Himmler that Hitler had given the order for a final solution to the Jewish question. In Hitler's words, according to Himmler, if the order was not carried out at that time, "then the Jews would later destroy the German people." Himmler also told him during this meeting that the final solution was to be regarded as a secret Reich matter; which meant that no one was to speak of it upon penalty of death. He was to tell no one of it - not even his immediate supervisor. Also bound to secrecy in this way were the sixty men who received the transports at the camps, which included all doctors and medical personnel.[77] The location of the Auschwitz concentration camp was chosen because of its isolation and its easy access by rail car.

> "Auschwitz was the most heavily guarded camp in Europe. The camp was a secret which the Nazis were determined would never be revealed, for once even a whisper about it escaped, the sheep would no longer walk quietly into the slaughterhouse."[78]

From a personal standpoint, I was shocked to learn that according to a witness named Dr. Wilhelm Hoettl, Eichmann told him that the final solution was known only to no more than 100 people.[79] Hoettl's testimony answered the question for me that is always asked about conspiratorial false flags and operations: How can so many people be involved and not say anything? First of all, it does not take a lot of people to plan and destroy the lives of millions if they have the power to do so and secondly, the ones involved are most likely blackmailed or held to the strictest secrecy on pain of death or maybe even something worse than death.

Upon their arrival to Auschwitz, the innocent victims were forced to surrender all their belongings and, for the ones who were not already naked during their transport, they were then forced to undress completely. After this initial degradation and humiliation, they were immediately sent to their deaths in the gas chambers under the pretense that they were to undergo a delousing or take a shower. When Hoess was asked if he felt guilty about what he did, given that he had a family and children of his own, he answered that his conscience did bother him at times. However, in spite of all the doubts he may have had, the only decisive argument for him was the strict order and the reason given for it by Himmler, ie. that the Jews were out to destroy the German people.[80]

This process of using manipulation, lies and terror was used to accomplish the holocaust by overriding the human conscience with an animal survival consciousness of personal self-interest. And of course, the secrecy aspect of it made no one the wiser to stop it.

As for our present day, when the leaders we elect make decisions in secret committee meetings, take testimony from witnesses behind closed doors, pass legislation at night or on weekends when no one is watching and add amendments to bills without debate or discussion, then we should all take notice. When they create agencies that require the secrecy of its employees, we should become scared. And when they openly conduct searches without probable cause in the name of national security, we can throw our hands up in defeat.

A war we never even knew about was declared behind closed doors and won in plain sight by re-branding the role of government from protecting its citizens from all threats, foreign and domestic, to one of protecting its citizens from all threats the government determines are threats under the umbrella motive of "in the interest of national security." There is a huge difference, and we are in it for the long-term I'm afraid. Just recently, I read about an 84-year-old man who was arrested for jay walking. Among the charges against him was a new one called "interference with governmental administration." Other than the fact that the charge can justify any action a government bureaucrat determines is negative, it also indicates that one of the last nails has been hammered into the coffin of liberty and freedom for all in America. Charges like that one give the authority to government officials to go after people they personally deem as threats to the state. It could conceivably cover someone who fails to pay a fine to the Bureau of Motor Vehicles on time, or even someone who fails to file their taxes on time.

Like the people who elected Hitler fully aware of the world

view he meticulously outlined in *Mein Kampf,* an electorate only has itself to blame for putting the focus on the external attributes of a candidate, like their charm or ability to speak well, while totally discounting the importance of that person's character.

10. False Assurances

Sometimes the giving of false assurances is way more effective than outright lying because it lulls the targets of your deception into doing exactly what you want them to do. False assurances give a person a false sense of security that a situation is about to improve and thereby keeps them from taking any proactive measures to help themselves while they still can.

Throughout 1939, Germany gave assurances over and over again to Belgium, Holland and Norway that it wanted peace and had no intention of invading. The reason Hitler did this was to lull the leaders of those countries into a false sense of security. If they knew that Hitler planned to invade them all along, they could have banded together with their European neighbors and allies to at least be able to put up some kind of fight when the inevitable happened. As it was, they were taken completely by surprise and overtaken by the Nazi regime in short order.[81]

The giving of false assurances was a tactic used repeatedly by Hitler and his foot soldiers. Konstantin von Neurath was a German diplomat who served as Foreign Minister of Germany between 1932 and 1938. It was revealed at his trial after the war that before the invasion of Czechoslovakia, he gave assurances that Germany would honor the terms of the German-Czechoslovak arbitration of 1925. As von Neurath was giving those assurances, he was well aware of Hitler's intention to invade Czechoslovakia based on a prior meeting he attended where the invasion was discussed.[82]

The word of Hitler and those in his inner circle willing to do his bidding meant absolutely nothing. However, by the time foreign leaders realized that fact, it was too late. As bad as those countries suffered as a result of their faith in treaties and the word of scoundrels, perhaps no group suffered worse consequences than the millions of Jews who relied on false assurances as they were led to their torture and death in the camps. Similar to the way they were taken from their homes with the false assurance they were being relocated, the Nazi soldiers got them into death vans by telling them it was to transport them to another location.[83]

If there is what we label evil in this world, this is it. It is using words to convey an intent that does not exist in reality. What we call evil always hides behind righteousness; otherwise, it would not achieve its goal. That is why it needs to be nipped in the bud as soon as we see the harmful intent behind the pleasant mask. That is the only way target(s) can take proactive action(s) to protect themselves.

As an environment becomes more accepting of the tactics adopted by Hitler from the Social Democrats, then it becomes more and more difficult to raise the alarm bell without getting harmed yourself. As I will discuss in the next chapter on creating the structure for the illusion, the system becomes rigged in favor of the illusion so that anyone who speaks up against it, is identified, isolated, and destroyed.

11. Deception (Use of Agent Provocateurs and Creating Fake Emergencies to Push Agenda Forward and Get Your Own People on Board (False Flags)

The Nazi government recruited criminals to commit murders that were made to appear as if they were committed by resistance organizations, in an attempt to dishonor those organizations. These types of operations took place in all the occupied countries. In Denmark, for instance, a series of murders were committed whereby high-profile people were shot while answering the door of their home, walking down the street or even during their doctor visits. Some were also killed in explosions. Although it was proven that these murders were committed through the coordinated efforts of Heinrich Himmler, Chief of the German Police/Gestapo and Guenther Pancke, Chief of Police in Denmark; signs like "Swine, you worked for Germany" were found on the bodies of the victims to make it appear that members of the resistance killed them.[84] Anyone not in the know would take the murders at face value and assume the murders were the work of the resistance fighters, rather than the work of governmental agent provocateurs seeking to damage the resistance in its efforts to overthrow Hitler and the Nazi party and get them out of their country.

Deception was a key component in pushing the agenda forward without making anyone the wiser. Hitler knew that the big changes he needed to make to the laws of the land at the time would not be possible in the environment of the Weimar Republic, where the Constitution gave freedom and equal rights to all German citizens. To consolidate his power and give him the authority he needed to institute his agenda, Hitler had to be able to take those rights from certain of the country's citizens. Rights are not easily taken from a free and sovereign people. An environment must be created where the free and sovereign people become willing to give up those rights voluntarily. That is where creating fake emergencies, otherwise known as false flag operations, come in very handy. The Reichstag fire and the incidents created to justify the invasion of foreign sovereign nations were used very effectively in convincing the German people that giving up their rights and going to war against nations who had done nothing to them was the right thing to do. Below is a synopsis of just three of those instances, although they were used throughout the rise and fall of the Third Reich.

11a. The Reichstag Fire

The Reichstag was the assembly location of the German parliament and it was a symbol of the free, parliamentary style of government Germany had under the Weimar Republic. On February 27, 1933, it burned down due to arson. Although it was highly likely that Nazi sympathizers started the fire, Hitler was successful in blaming the fire on the Communists.

As was fairly well proven at the Nuremberg trials, the Reichstag fire was a false flag operation blamed on the Communists and used by Hitler to make the German people think there was a threat to their national security. The Presidential Emergency Decree of February 28, 1933, was signed the day after the Reichstag fire [which means it was researched, drafted and written at some time before the fire]. The decree provided the basis for imprisoning people without judicial proceedings – the process known as protective custody.

Hitler also took advantage of the hysteria caused by his trumped up threat of a Communist revolution to get The Law for the Protection of the People and the Reich of March 24, 1933 passed. Also known as the Enabling Act, the law provided Hitler with powers that allowed him to defund all the independent German states, put them under his control without any struggle and then appoint Nazi governors who were all subject to the central authority of the Reich Minister of the Interior.

The Enabling Act was responsible for nullifying many of the key civil liberties German citizens enjoyed under the Weimar Constitution. With Nazis in powerful positions in the German government, the law was used as the legal basis for the imprisonment of anyone considered to be an opponent of the Nazi agenda. It was also used to suppress publications not considered 'friendly' to the Nazi cause. The decree is considered by historians as one of the first key steps in the establishment of a one-party Nazi state in Germany.[85]

The leadership corps of the N.S.D.A.P. possessed absolute power and control in Germany. Hitler used this absolute power to destroy civil liberties under the guise that he was doing it "in the interest of public security and order."[86] Protective custody provided Hitler with a means for rounding up the Communists and Social Democrats and placing them in concentration camps. It was not long before protective custody was being used to round up "political prisoners, Jews, anti-socials, gypsies, felons, homosexuals and before 1937, also the Bible researchers."[87] The anti-socials were anyone who was determined to be a danger to the State and security of the people because of their attitude.[88] The prosecutors at Nuremberg viewed protective custody as the terrible power to imprison people without judicial proceedings and often without charges or any indication as to the length of detainment.[89]

11b. False Flag Incident Used to Invade Czechoslovakia

The Nazi leadership told the Czechoslovak government that they would not attack Czechoslovakia,[90] but within a month, they were holding planning meetings for the attack. One such meeting took place on April 21, 1938, at which they talked about creating an incident that would justify the invasion. One possible incident discussed was to assassinate their own German ambassador at Prague. Although they ultimately decided against the assassination, they continued holding meetings throughout the months of May, June, July, August and September to further refine their plans for attack.

11c. False Flag Incident Used to Invade Poland

Hitler liked using false flag incidents to justify invasions of foreign countries. The planned incident for invading Poland was named "Operation Himmler." It was one of the more bizarre, yet violent, incidents used by Hitler's gang. They planned a fake attack on a German radio station using concentration camp inmates dressed in Polish army uniforms so that the attack could be blamed on Poland. The inmates were given fatal injections, then they were shot and their dead bodies were placed outside the radio station to make it appear like they had been killed while attacking and infiltrating the station.[91] A fake speech purported to be given by one of the attackers was aired in Polish saying the time had come for war against the Germans and telling the Poles they should get together and kill any Germans who resisted.

12. Compartmentalization/Need to Know

Wilhelm Keitel, Chief of the Armed Forces High Command, testified at trial that Hitler abused his authority with regard to the generals in a fundamental way that prevented them from acting in accordance with their sense of right and wrong. It was through a process called compartmentalization.

Hitler's No. 1 order, as Keitel called it, was a way to compartmentalize information so that the knowledge of each general and his subordinates was limited in such a way as to prevent any one person from seeing the overall picture. In essence, the order was as follows:

1. No one shall know about secret matters which do not belong to his own range of assignments.

2. No one shall learn more than he needs to fulfill the tasks assigned to him.

3. No one shall receive information earlier than is necessary for the performance of the duties assigned to him.

4. No one shall transmit orders which are to be kept secret to subordinate offices to any greater extent or any earlier than is unavoidable for the achievement of the purpose.[92]

Up until the time of his trial after the war, Keitel claimed he was operating with limited knowledge due to the Nazi practice of compartmentalizing information. It was not until he was given access to all the documents at his trial that he became aware of everything that had taken place behind closed doors and it was his testimony that the army generals would have been proactive if they had been given the full picture of what was being done in the occupied territories.

Also, as previously mentioned, the final solution (the operation to exterminate the Jews) was a special Reich secret that was known of by only a few people. Hoettl himself did not learn of it until the end of August, 1944 when he received information about it directly from Eichmann himself.[93] Similarly, very few people knew of the medical experiments that took place at the camps, and of those who did know, if they said anything about them they were killed.[94]

I do not say this to mitigate their crimes in any way, but it is very hard to act with awareness and make good choices when you are not given all the facts of a situation. That is precisely why Hitler decided to set up the structure in a way where information could be kept compartmentalized; with each person knowing just enough to do their job but not enough to take proactive measures, as Keitel claimed he would have done had he known the full extent of what was being carried out in all the occupied territories. As it was, "as these atrocities developed one out of the other, step by step and without any foreknowledge of the consequences, destiny took its tragic course with fateful results."[95]

13. Keeping Up Appearances

Although the moral degenerates were the cream of the crop in the illusory Republic called Nazi Germany, they did not wear their degeneracy on their sleeves. The false appearances Hitler's leadership corps presented to the public in no way resembled the people they actually were. You know the saying, 'appearances can be deceiving.' Perhaps more accurately, it can be said that appearances can be manipulated. In a narcissistic and egoistic society, the tendency is to judge people based on outward appearances. It is possibly the most dangerous aspect of the illusion because it sets up a victim up for abuse and in many cases, it prevents justice from being done.

In an illusory environment, the self image called reputation (how one appears to the external world) is far more important than one's internal character. A CEO who appeared in a documentary on the 2008 economic downturn, so beautifully summed up the culture that created the men who surrounded Hitler when he said he was more concerned with reputation than conscience. Reputations are built and die in the short term. They are as illusory as the fake structures they rely on for their sustainability and still, people will lie, betray, deceive and destroy to protect them.

It is very easy to create a reputation in this world. It is much more difficult to acquire and retain character. Many cruel and unethical people are pillars of the community. They receive awards from presidents and start charitable foundations, but will destroy a colleague for speaking her mind or steal from people who trust them to enrich themselves.

Information is not the only thing that can be

compartmentalized. A person's character can be as well. People love to hide behind reputation. That is why it is so hard for us to believe that a successful person who has done so much good for the community is capable of committing horrendous acts in the other compartments of their life.

Avner Less, the police officer who interrogated Adolf Eichmann after his capture in Argentina, said that Adolf Eichmann, the man responsible for the killing of millions of Jews in the final solution, bore no resemblance to the monster he had envisioned in his mind. The monster turned out to be a skinny, ordinary looking man with a wife and kids. I think it is safe to say that most all of Hitler's leadership corps were ordinary looking men who had wives and children. There was certainly nothing in their outward appearances to indicate that they were capable of committing the horrific war crimes for which they were accused. Yet even still, this hardened police officer who had probably seen it all was still taken by surprise by how unassuming one of the worst offenders appeared to him.[96]

Hans Frank, the Governor General of Poland after its occupation, was an accomplished lawyer and the father of five children. Outwardly, he appeared to be the most cultured and refined among Hitler's bevy of misfits. However, inwardly he was among the worst of them. His personal diary was confiscated upon his capture and it revealed that the cultured father of five was, in truth, a blood thirsty killer of men and women. He had no regard for the Poles he was charged with leading and, in fact, declared the day after assuming his duties as Governor General of Poland that the Poles "shall be the slaves of the German Reich." It was also Frank who was placed in charge of an operation code-named 'Extraordinary Pacification Action.' The purpose of the operation was to rid Poland of all its intelligentsia per Hitler's orders that all men capable of leadership in Poland were to be eliminated. When all was said and done, this accomplished father of five was responsible for rounding up and killing 3,500 of Poland's best and brightest of lights.[97]

Hermann Goering was one of the most powerful Nazi leaders until the ending years of the war when he fell out of favor with Hitler. There is a reason for his meteoric rise to power within the party and it had nothing to do with either talent or integrity. He was a favored member of Hitler's team largely because of the respectability, credibility and personal connections he provided to Hitler. Among those connections were Prince Philip of Hesse, who had married Princess Mafalda, the daughter of the King of Italy; Fritz Thyssen, head of the Thyssen mining and steelmaking company, and other barons of the business world, as well as a number of prominent Army officers.[98]

Unlike the other moral degenerates who comprised most of Hitler's leadership corps, Ernst Kaltenbrunner, leader of the Austrian SS and subsequently head of all police forces in Nazi Germany, came from a prominent family. His prominence and substantial appearance made him one of the most dangerous men in the corps because he used his outward affability and charm to conceal his "core of steel, his vindictiveness, his cruelty, his lust for self-adornment, self-glorification and power."[99] The foreign nations who depended on him to tell them the true intentions of the Nazi Party had no idea of the man behind the mask with whom they were dealing – much to their own detriment.[100]

As for Adolf Hitler himself, Volume 1 of *Mein Kampf* was published in 1925 and Volume 2 in 1926. That was more than a decade before WWII. In it, Hitler makes clear his hatred for the Jews and his belief that they were the cause of all of society's ills. He was clear about who he was and what he wanted to do. By the time the people who voted him into office glimpsed the society they themselves helped him create, they were all too fearful to do anything about it. They could have made different choices – harder choices – and worked through their country's problems in more constructive ways than putting a demented dictator in charge, but he was charismatic and told them what they wanted to hear. He also gave them much of what they wanted, but at what price? I can answer that. The price of their humanity.

To this day, we continue to be taken in by a person's outward appearance. All our politicians have beautiful families they parade out at all the campaign stops, as if to say having a family makes them good people. Corporate executives love to keep family photos on their desk and exchange in friendly banter about their kids. We just cannot imagine how such good family men who are so devoted to their kids can be so ruthless when it comes to performing their jobs.

Scott Peck, author of *People of the Lie: The Hope for Healing Human Evil*, talks about how evil will very rarely expose itself to public light. It must hide. And it almost always hides under the guise of something righteous. "In fact, rather than hiding in the shadows dressed in black, it disguises itself in suits, uniforms, and charitable organizations, which allow it to deceive us into thinking it's our savior. This enables it to cause far greater damage."

We have learned how not to judge a book by its cover. Before plunking down our $10.99, we will read the flap and all the customer reviews to make sure it is worth buying. Now we need to learn how to do the same kind of analysis with people. The only way to expose the person behind the mask is to rip off the mask. We need to do that by recognizing the patterns of deception that indicate a person is putting up a front and take affirmative action to call them out for their deception.

Chapter 5
Creating the Structure
for the Illusion

1. Authority (and Obedience to)
1a. Swearing an Oath

During his testimony at Nuremberg, Wilhelm Keitel, Chief of the German Armed Forces High Command, gave a very cogent explanation for why he executed the criminal orders of Hitler, even though he admitted that some of the orders caused him to have a serious conflict of conscience knowing the consequences they would have. In the end, it all came down to what he felt was his duty as a soldier of the Third Reich. As a soldier, it never, ever entered his mind to revolt against the head of the State and the Supreme Commander of the Armed Forces.[101]

Hitler knew there would be men like Keitel, whose consciences would bother them having to do the things they were ordered to do. That is why one of the first moves he made after taking over as Head of State and Commander in Chief of the Armed Forces, was to have the soldiers swear an oath to him rather than to Germany and its Constitution. The oath read as follows: "I swear by God this sacred oath, that I will render unconditional obedience to Adolf Hitler, the Fuehrer of the German Reich and people, Supreme Commander of the

Armed Forces, and will be ready as a brave soldier to risk my life at any time for this oath."[102] After taking that oath, it became almost impossible to disobey an order without risking court martial and/or one's life. It was a fateful choice each of them made, but it was a choice nonetheless.[103]

As William Shirer pointed out in his book, prior to that time the generals could have easily overthrown the regime. However, once they tied themselves to Hitler through that oath, they were honor-bound to obey him. Although some of the orders bothered the consciences of a few of the generals, the oath itself provided them with a justification for their actions and relieved more than a few of them of feeling any responsibility for the consequences of carrying out those orders. [104]

2. Entitlement (the Elite with a Master-Slave Mentality (Us vs. Them)

Back when I was still watching television news programs, there would often be a commentator talking about the hypocrisy of this or that politician. I would be disgusted by the hypocrisy, but the politicians they were talking about were never held to account, nothing was ever done about it and life just moved on as before. After studying Hitler, I now realize how politicians and other power players can be so flagrant about their hypocrisy. Other than the fact they get away with it, they know that the system holds an underlying assumption of which the rest of us are made unaware and that assumption is that there are two sets of rules; one for them and one for everyone else. In their minds, they have done nothing wrong or hypocritical because their behavior gets judged by a different standard. That is why a universal healthcare law can be passed, which is meant to be applied to everyone [hence the word 'universal'], yet the government officials who passed the law are allowed to have healthcare policies outside the regulations of the law and the rest of the population must comply with the law. In such situations, the creators of the laws make themselves above the law. I am certain their reasoning is that the creator of a thing is not bound by the requirements of the thing, since the creator is outside and above the thing. In creating laws, our legislators too often feel that they are creating the laws for their constituents and not for themselves. It is a kind of us vs. them mentality. However, this mentality is not limited to healthcare laws [and yes, it is hypocrisy in countries where there are written documents stating all people are equal under the law]. It affects tax laws; national security laws; financial, economic and behavioral laws; and unwritten rules at every level of society. It is why corporate executives can get their kids' college education paid for by the companies where they work while many of their employees' kids have to endure years of debt to pay for it; why lawyers in law firms can get free parking and other kinds of perks denied to the workers lower on the totem pole; why college presidents and business executives can obtain exemptions from airport security while the rest of us have to schlep through long lines and endure multiple levels of checks, etc., etc. etc.

Hitler knew this mindset very well. He could justify rewriting his country's Constitution and laws to make them more in line with his own personal agenda because he held what he called a folk concept of the world. Hitler believed that the human race was being led through stages to reach a higher type of human – what the philosopher, Fredrich Nietzsche, called the 'superman'. Once this superman status is achieved, Hitler believed this higher race of mankind would possess the entire earth and "be free to work in every domain all over the world and even reach spheres that lie outside the earth." At that time, these superior CEO's of the world would be destined to become the masters of all people in the world and they would have "at their disposal all the means and resources of the whole world."[105]

Hitler viewed himself as one of these supermen. I think the sense of entitlement he had runs through corrupted minds the world over because of the hierarchical systems that feed it. Giving someone the title of CEO, president, senator, vice president, etc. and perching them on top of some theoretical hierarchy etched on paper naturally gives them a sense that they are on top looking down on all the rows of people below them. When that mindset gets reinforced by actions that protect them from being punished for wrongdoing by people at the same level of the hierarchy or higher, then the mindset gets ingrained not only in their minds, but also in the minds of the people at the bottom of the hierarchy who come to see it as just the way things are and there is nothing to be done about it.

Hitler believed that humanity would eventually be faced with problems that only this higher race of elite would be equipped to overcome. I call this higher race of elite the Chief Executive Officers of the world, but Hitler referred to them as 'masters of the world.' His use of the word *master* for these men is very intentional because it implies that the rest of humanity would be put in the position of being their slaves.

> "In the New Order which he began to impose on the Slavs in the East during the war, the Czechs, the Poles, the Russians were—and were to remain, if the grotesque New Order had endured - the hewers of wood and the drawers of water for their German masters."[106]

Holding the philosophy he did, it was natural for Hitler to believe that "the world is not there to be possessed by the faint-hearted races." Therefore, he went forward doing his best to enslave and murder the Slavs, Poles and Russians of eastern Europe; plundering their resources in order to give them to the superior German race he was creating at home; who would then become the vice presidents, directors, general managers and security detail in the new world order he was hell bent on creating.[107]

3. Hierarchy/Hitler's Leadership Principle

Much of the ugliness of the human mind arises from the unnatural and man-made hierarchies that designate some human beings as more valuable than other human beings. Hierarchies conflict with purpose and destiny. However, the pyramidal model of control that hierarchy provides is the best structure in which corrupt people can operate. The structure allows power to coalesce at the top where dictator/tyrant/CEO/group can direct all the handpicked minions on the rows below in how to institute the policies.

Charismatic and corrupt leaders are able to seize control of people's minds by putting a hierarchical structure of people in place that spreads their personal ideology from the man at the top to the managers in the rows below and then out to the masses at the bottom. Anyone caught not conforming to the message is punished or exterminated. Punishment can take the form of career assassination, destruction of one's reputation, shunning, harassment, threats of harm to the family, imprisonment or even murder. Unless they are extremely naive and believe that people are basically good and incapable of cruelty toward people they know and like, most individuals catch on very quickly that the only rules that count are those of the leader and all other values, rules and laws are merely smoke screens the leaders hide behind to give a false impression to the rest of the world.

It was Hitler's view that there should never be majority decisions – only persons of authority. The pyramidal structure of hierarchy allowed for the placing of authority in the hands of one man at each level of the pyramid to make decisions, while having many councilors and advisers by his side to advise him on those decisions. Eventually, absolute responsibility combined with absolute authority would breed <u>an elite set of leaders</u> that would rule the world he planned on conquering.[108]

Centralization of information was made possible because the entire government and society in Hitler's Germany was structured hierarchically. The power of the pyramidal control grid extended out over all phases of public and private life. Like his other strategies for power and control, Hitler adopted his leadership principle from what he saw as the Social Democratic authoritarianism of the Prussian Army, where leadership was directed downward, and responsibility went upward. He found that hierarchy was really the best structure for achieving his agenda to undermine Parliament and coalesce power in his hands. Knowing that he could not dispense with Parliament entirely, he subverted the institution by making it a working institution rather than a voting institution.

Hitler structured the German society in a hierarchical structure as well for purposes of controlling it. The country was divided into districts, or Gaue, at the head of which was a gauleiter appointed by Hitler. A Gaue was further subdivided into Kreise, each of which was governed by a Kreisleiter. The Kreise was then subdivided into smaller local groups called Ortsgruppes. The Ortsgruppes were were then divided into local street cells and blocks, which had blockleiters reporting back on the activities of the individual citizen.[109]

Powerful people are very strategic in their own ways. Totalitarian and other authoritarian organizations and governments will generously reimburse people in management to get them to conform their actions to the agenda of the people in the top row of the hierarchy. For instance, in communist and other totalitarian and fascist regimes, this management structure translates to the government bureaucrats, military and police force. The jobs in the enforcement branches are given to the disenfranchised and under-educated because their lack of skills and education make them unemployable in the private sector and therefore very malleable in what they are willing to do because of their limited options. It is in the best interests of a corrupt ruling class to always keep a portion of the population disenfranchised and unhappy because that becomes its pool of employees.

I watched a documentary on the military regime that ruined Burma and the people who live there. Massive wealth lives side-by-side with the worst poverty on the planet. People there are working to get one meal a day. They interviewed young children who wanted to go to school so badly. Instead, they are working in sweat shops to help feed their families one meal a day. There is little to no electricity. The houses are shacks. The military is the only means for young men to make a living. The government takes the children that they refuse to educate and puts them in the military where they propagandize them into abusing, spying on and suppressing the population. These young men feel such loyalty to the military which has given them a means of support that they are more than willing to do what is asked of them. It is so diabolical when societal constructs are rigged in this manner. It turns everything upside-down and makes us grateful to people who have hijacked our bodies and souls for their own personal gain.

4. Spies/Citizen Informants

The blockleiter in Nazi Germany had neighbors spying on neighbors and reporting their activities to the local S.S. These people did not become spies overnight. Hitler and Goebbels created a massive propaganda machine that touched every area of German society. By the time they began rounding up Jews in the Final Solution, these members of the blockleiter thought that what they were doing was right. In their propagandized consciousness, the Jews were the villains who had caused all of Germany's problems. Hitler always framed the persecution of the Jews in terms of handling the Jewish problem. All power abusers and bullies portray their targets of abuse as the problem in the relationship and then use their more powerful position in the relationship to convince everyone else that the target is the problem as well. A non-conscious population that does the cost-benefit analysis based upon their external environment, rather than any internal set of values and rules that they will not compromise, is easily convinced by the people in power who control the information flow and can pass laws that make it detrimental not to conform to the party line.

As any parent knows, there are two tried and true approaches for getting your children to do something you want them to do: the carrot and the stick. The carrot and stick is a metaphor for the use of reward (carrot) or punishment (stick) to obtain a desired behavior. In a time where the FBI routinely uses the carrot and stick approach to induce citizens to become informants, such as threatening an offender with re-incarceration or paying a person to snitch; it is good to remember that there was a time when this behavior was considered abhorrent. One of the prosecutors at the Nuremberg trials said, "I have frequently shown that, in their determination to impose their reign of terror, the Germans resorted to means which revolt the human conscience. Of these, one of the most repugnant is inducement to become informers."[110] It makes one wonder how far we have come in what we will assault our consciences with and still feel good about ourselves in our own 21st century 'war on terror' where spies are not called blockleiter, but instead are called alert citizens who if they see something, are to say something! The FBI calls them informants and the CIA refers to them as assets.

There were 'alert citizens,' informants, assets, spies and snitches everywhere in Hitler's Germany, where the average citizen was decent, albeit intimidated, and resistance was successfully forced underground.

> "Everywhere, in the Ministries and Chancelleries, in private dwellings and in restaurants there were alert citizens who, out of fanaticism or for pay, were willing to report everything they saw and heard."[111]

Even the electoral process was tainted and compromised through techniques used by the SD, which was the intelligence agency in Nazi Germany. The SD was comprised of agents and informants who operated in the administrative/regional offices of the Reich, and later, in conjunction with the Gestapo and police in the occupied territories. The mission of the SD was to bring every single individual within the Third Reich's reach under continuous supervision. The prosecutors at Nuremberg officially declared the SD a criminal organization, along with the Gestapo (the police arm of the Nazi regime) and the SS (the private army of the regime).[112] In short, the Gestapo was the terror arm of the Nazi regime and the SD was the spying arm that spied upon people in the streets, in shops, and even in churches. However, one of the more detestable tasks they performed was to secretly mark ballots for purposes of identifying peoples' votes.[113]

5. Redefine the Law and Constitution to Suit Objectives

In his testimony at trial, Hermann Goering, the second most powerful man in Nazi Germany, gave away how power players feel about laws. When asked if the aims of the N.S.D.A.P. agenda were to be achieved by every means, even if illegal means, he replied, "Of course they were to be achieved by every means. The conception 'illegal' should, perhaps, be clarified. If I aim at a revolution, then it is an illegal action for the State then in existence. If I am successful, then it becomes a fact and thereby legal."[114]

To people like Goering, what is legal and what is not is dependent on the people in power. It is therefore not surprising that one of the first acts Hitler took when he assumed power was to pass the Enabling Act of 1935. Essentially, the Enabling Act gave him the right to alter Germany's Constitution. Under this act, the German parliament (Reichstag) had to turn its constitutional functions over to Hitler. By doing so, Hitler was given the right to alter the Constitution. His alterations of the Constitution, along with the Presidential Emergency Decree of February 28, 1933, that nullified many civil liberties of the German citizens, gave Hitler free reign over Germany.[115]

Hitler needed the ability to change the country's Constitution and thereby turn it into a 'living document' so that he could move forward with an agenda that was in direct conflict with the civil liberties and protections that Germany's Constitution provided to the German citizen. He needed a document that could easily be changed to fit any situation.

Objective standards like those found in a country's Constitution are so vital for this reason and must be upheld at all times. External conditions in our world do change and that is exactly the reason why we need a constant set of values that do not change. They give us a standard we can use to guide our actions as we navigate changing circumstances, as well as provide us with indicators to show us when a person is trying to deceive us into a course of action we should not take.

Hitler made Germany's Constitution a living document that could be changed so that he could make some people and groups more secure than others. It allowed him to pass new laws when existing ones got in the way of his agenda. The holocaust could never have happened if Hitler had not been allowed to turn Germany's Constitution into a living document that could be altered at will, because in the hands of men like Adolf Hitler and Josef Goebbels, Constitutions and the rule of law do not provide security for the people. They love the idea of living documents that can be changed to suit any situation or agenda. Goebbels said as much in a speech he gave on October, 1935, where he stated, "The Jewish question will not be solved separately, but by laws which we enact for we are the anti-Jewish Government."[116]

Changing the Constitution allowed Hitler to pass laws that excluded certain groups from society for purposes of targeting and eliminating them. From my point of view, passing laws that divide people into groups for any purpose is a dangerous practice because a protected group can always become a targeted group if they begin to pose a threat to the power structure; or if in the case of Hitler, the authoritarian at the top row of the power pyramid has taken a personal disliking to them. I have yet to find an instance of any kind of abuse that does not have its roots in the abuse of power. Abusive practices - from slavery, child abuse, human trafficking, racism, bullying, discrimination, mobbing, murder, rape, police brutality, female mutilation, and on and on – always arise out of some person or group having control over another person or group and the willingness to abuse that power of control to serve their own self-interests. The only way the rights of the group can be protected is by protecting the rights of the individual. That has always been true and will always be true.

6. Corporate - Government Alliance

In the structure created by Hitler, people were dependent on the corrupt government when they took a corporate job because Hitler took control of private industry and put it under the Nazi umbrella. The conservatives in Nazi Germany were the industrialists who supported Hitler. Hitler required huge sums of money to finance election campaigns, pay for the widespread propaganda, fund the war machine, pay the hundreds of bureaucrats in the hierarchy and maintain the private armies of the SA and SS. In order to raise those sums, he cultivated relationships with rich industrialists. Despite the victory of Hitler and the N.S.D.A.P. at the polls, it was the conservative industrialists who held the purse strings. Their wealth was used to help Hitler combat the Communists, Socialists and trade unions. William Shirer wrote, "So hush-hush were some of [the meetings Hitler had with industrialists] that they had to be held "in some lonely forest glade." Privacy was essential in these matters so that the press would not get wind of it and expose the cushy arrangement between Hitler and his corporate enablers. And in the end, privacy served them well. Many of the secret dealings were never exposed until the trials that took place after the war.[117] In addition, the prosecutors at Nuremberg provided evidence that German corporations and financiers aided and abetted Heinrich Himmler, the Reich leader of the S.S., in his subjugation, exploitation, oppression and destruction of people both in Germany and the countries Germany invaded.[118]

Corporate wealth was used to subsidize both the Nazi Party and the political press that so effectively spread the Nazi propaganda.[119] I have no doubt that the creation of the corporate/fascist structure in Nazi Germany served well in silencing the majority of the population who were dependent on that structure for their financial well-being. It certainly would have made one think twice before coming to the aid of an innocent colleague who was being detained without charge and put into protective custody; or worse, taken to a concentration camp just for being who they were.

People like Hitler are very much aware of this dynamic and use it until every good, courageous and decent person is frightened into submission for fear of losing everything they have if they rock the boat of corruption. It makes change very hard, if not impossible, once an entire environment becomes corrupt in such a way that good people no longer see the benefit in speaking out against the illusion.

7. Theft of resources (usually the reason for war)

Thievery was given the stamp of approval in Germany by creating government offices in charge of handling the distribution of the stolen items. In foreign countries, these offices would receive requisitions for items needed by Germany industry. The requisitioned machines and materials would then be shipped to Germany. Official gangs of thugs were put in charge of looting, dismantling and transporting the equipment.[120] In addition to machines and materials, land was also stolen. The SS confiscated Polish farmland and distributed it to German inhabitants. The owners of the land were then employed as laborers or deported to Germany against their will and forced into labor.[121]

All the scientific institutions, libraries and museums in Russia were ransacked and everything was transported to Germany.[122] Also, all the raw material, food and other supplies needed to maintain the German war machine were pillaged from Russia and sent to Germany.[123] Likewise, with the country of Holland, which was one of the wealthiest countries in Europe. Rich in resources and food, Holland and its people were almost entirely ruined by the Nazi invaders. When the Allies liberated the country four years after the German occupation, they found the population starved.[124]

Although Hitler liked to claim that he liberated the countries he took over, his goal was always to settle those countries and use their land and resources to benefit Germany. His true goal was made clear at a conference held at his headquarters on July 16, 1941; where he told the attendees that Germany's objectives in the East were to "dominate it, administer it and exploit it."[125]

Hitler saw the acquisition of "agricultural territories" as the only means for solving Germany's economic needs.[126] He was incapable of looking at solutions for those needs through the lens of trade and commerce because of his 'survival of the fittest', 'only the strong survive', and 'might makes right' consciousness. It was out of this consciousness that he created Germany's war machine. He needed to invade Poland, Czechoslovakia, Austria and Russia to acquire the food resources and labor pool needed to maintain that war machine and keep the war economy going.[127]

In the case of Russia, he planned on starving millions of its people by diverting its products to Germany, seizing the livestock for use by Germany and establishing a priority by which the food produced would be allocated: first, to the combat troops, then the troops in foreign territories, then the troops stationed in Germany, then the German civilian population and lastly, to the populations of the occupied countries.[128] In all the occupied territories, Germany followed a policy of enrichment through theft, debased currencies, extraction of loans, imposition of occupation levies, exacting financial contributions and issuing occupation currency far in excess of occupation costs. The excess was then used to purchase business properties and supplies in the occupied countries.[129]

8. The Use of Terrorism to Subdue the Public

Gerhart H. Segar was a peace activist and a representative of the Social Democratic Party. According to his affidavit, submitted as evidence at the Nuremberg trials, the Nazis considered terrorism to be a necessary and desirable weapon in their efforts to destroy democratic opposition.*130* The Nazis labeled him and all Communists as terrorists and threw them all into concentration camps. In fact, the concentration camps were originally built for the Communists, not the Jews. Another group of peace activists put into protective custody in the concentration camps were the Jehovah's Witnesses. The reason given for their detention was that it was a preventative measure in the interest of national security.[131]

Likewise, the Nazis also used the false charge of 'terrorism' to subdue the populations in the countries they conquered. Protective custody and Germany's internment camps were ruthlessly used for the sole purpose of annihilating and exterminating the perceived enemies of the Nazi state; while at the same time, "creating a system of terror, which it exploited to facilitate the realisation of its political aims."[132]

Hate speech was included within the terrorism paradigm the Nazis used to accuse their enemies of crimes. Anyone caught making "spiteful statements inimical to Germany" were also placed in concentration camps.[133] There was only one acceptable way to think in Nazi Germany and anyone voicing a different opinion was considered a dissident. Terror, violence and incarceration were the means used to silence dissident voices so that the Nazis could consolidate their power over the German people.[134] Included in speech that was considered 'spiteful statements inimical to Germany' was any talk about "loyalty to God, church and scientific truth."[135]

Even the leadership corps of the N.S.D.A.P. did not escape the speech patrol. Anyone expressing an opinion Hitler didn't want to hear could easily have found himself shot. At the very least, that person was labeled a demoralizing influence who crushed the hope and happiness of all the men comprising Hitler's leadership corps.[136]

However, the Nazi terrorism was not without limits. Before

implementing their agenda of aggressive warfare, the Nazis did experiments to test the resolve of the resistance, always ready to draw back if they got the feeling the public temperament was against them.[137] The persecution of the Jews was one such experiment. Hitler knew he would face resistance in all the countries he invaded, and he needed a way to repress that resistance as much as possible. The Jewish ghetto was the laboratory for testing repressive measures.

The techniques of targeting, intimidation, manipulation, deceit, destruction, terror and the host of other methods Hitler used to subdue the public and bring them into compliance with his will had the effect of destroying all human decency and courage. "Open resistance, which was never more than feeble, all but disappeared. The little resistance that existed was forced underground. At that point, the Nazis had the German state firmly in their grip."[138]

PART II – REALITY

Chapter 6
The Fallacy of the Greater
Good Rationalization

Hitler was seventeen years old when he was unjustly terminated from two jobs in Vienna because he expressed unpopular political views with his socialist colleagues. Since employment is the means most of us have for financially surviving in this world, it is an extremely traumatic event to get terminated from a job. If on top of that, the termination is an unfair and unjust one, it can eat away at us. I have absolutely no doubt that at the heart of many workplace shootings are people who perceive their terminations were for unjust reasons. And since at that point they really have no recourse against the company, they take their anger and unresolved feelings of resentment and hate out in a violent manner against their co-workers.

It is a fact that every person has an innate belief as a human being with a consciousness that they have the right to self-determine what they do with their bodies and minds. When the perpetrators of abuse destroy that true assumption by forcibly taking over control from their victims' bodies and/or minds by emotionally and/or physically abusing them, they steal that person's sense of self confidence and identity as a human being possessed with the right to self-determine their own destiny. It is like splitting a person apart at their core. The buildup of hatred, confusion, anger, frustration and feelings of hopelessness and helplessness at not being able to do anything about it are beyond comprehension. I do not agree with school shooters, but I certainly understand where they are coming from when they are targets of bullying that is never resolved. Revenge is a very powerful motive for people who have had their consciousness harmed in such an intentional and malicious manner. It is an easy way to take back control — at least for the moment. Then, of course, if they do not kill themselves, the system takes all control from them forever.

Revenge may seem satisfying on any battlefield, but it is a self-defeating strategy in the long-term that causes far worse harm than the original harm it is meant to avenge. The far better choice for the human targets of power abusers is to have faith in the laws of cause and effect to which the human consciousness is bound. Control over one's own body and mind can only be restored by putting all of one's personal energy into doing the kinds of things that focus on healing themselves. That is the time, more than any other time in one's life, to concentrate on Jesus's first commandment to love God with all your heart, soul and mind. [See Matthew 22:36] I believe this commandment encompasses the whole of loving the eternal consciousness labeled as God and loving ourselves as an extension of that consciousness on this physical plane. Loving oneself involves protecting the sanctity of one's consciousness.

This is my own theory, and I really do not know if it is true or not, but it is my opinion that trauma destroys the ego consciousness, so that after trauma, the ego reasserts itself stronger than ever as a means of restoration of the person one was before the trauma. The fact is, a person will never be the same after trauma so that restoration of the same ego consciousness one had before is an impossible task. The dissociation many persons experience is the consciousness not knowing how to feel or think after experiencing the loss of the ego. The key to healing is to not to try to restore the ego consciousness from before, but rather, to create a new consciousness that is stronger and wiser and is able to figure out how to incorporate the traumatic experience into a new world view. Healing is all about transformation, not restoration.

Concentrating on oneself to the exclusion of everyone else when it is required for personal health and well-being is not selfish. It is, in fact, God's way of protecting its own consciousness on this physical plane. In *Mein Kampf*, Hitler wrote that he suffered great mental anguish after the job terminations and he blamed his Marxist work colleagues for causing it. Instead of taking his anger out on the co-workers responsible, he took it out on all people like them who adopted the ideas of Social Democracy. As mentioned earlier, the concentration camps were built for the sole purpose of rounding up and incarcerating the Social Democrats. One would think Hitler would have healed himself from the trauma by the time he came to power in Germany; however, I think it was probably due to Hitler's obstinacy that he was able to hold on to the mental anguish and anger of a seventeen-year old boy until he held the power to rid Germany of what that mentally tortured young man saw as the "ever-increasing and menacing army of people who could no longer be reckoned as belonging to their own nation."[139]

It wasn't until he found out that some of the owners of the newspapers pushing the Social Democratic ideas were Jewish that he began the character assassination of all Jews in his own mind.[140]

For a number of convoluted pages in *Mein Kampf*, Hitler goes through a bevy of justifications, rationalizations and lies his mind used to create a species of sub-human Jews out a group of people he claims to have never given much thought to while growing up.[141]

First, he noticed how they dressed differently and smelled bad – not at all like all the other German citizenry.[142] Then he concluded that the Jews were responsible for the moral degradation he saw in the cultural activities in Germany. He felt they were responsible for what he saw as "the hideous productions of the cinema and theatre.[143] Then when he somehow concluded that the Jews were primarily responsible for prostitution and the white human slave trade, his wrath became such that he committed himself to bringing "the Jewish problem to light in all its details."[144] According to him though, the final straw came when he realized that the Jews were the leaders of the Social Democratic movement. It was then that the scales fell from his eyes and he realized that the Jew was the evil alien leading the German people astray with its Communist (Social Democratic) doctrine. He writes:

> "It was that this alien race held in its hands the leadership of that Social Democratic Party with whose minor representatives I had been disputing for months past. I was happy at last to know for certain that the Jew is not a German. Thus I finally discovered who were the evil spirits leading our people astray."[145]

It was not enough for Hitler to just hate the men who made him miserable. He had to turn them and those who held the same views as them into Satan-loving aliens leading the world astray. He concludes the chapter with the following passage:

> "Should the Jew, with the aid of his Marxist creed, triumph over the people of this world, his Crown will be the funeral wreath of mankind, and this planet will once again follow its orbit through ether, without any human life on its surface, as

it did millions of years ago. And so I believe to-day that my
conduct is in accordance with the will of the Almighty
Creator. In standing guard against the Jew I am defending the
handiwork of the Lord."[146]

Hitler gave us the benefit of taking a glimpse into the workings
of his mind. He showed us how a person can go from assumption A to
assumption Z without any logical means for doing so. According to
him, he went from thinking not at all about Jews while growing up in
Linz to thinking that if the Jews and their Marxist creed were allowed
to continue on, it would mean the end of all mankind. Therefore, he
concluded it was his calling from God to save the world from such a
menace. What his change of thinking illustrates to me is that Hitler first
justified the holocaust in his own mind before creating a huge
propaganda machine to convince others of the rightness of his
justification.

In a similar way, the chief priest Caiaphas, who was responsible
for putting out the death order for Jesus, tells his Pharisee underlings
who will be doing the dirty work that if Jesus is allowed to continue
preaching to the Jews, it will be the end of the nation. Make no mistake
about it, Jesus was sentenced to death long before his arrest and
farcical trial and the sentence was imposed due largely to the
rationalizations of Caiaphas, the chief priest. In John, chapter 11, it
says that many of the Jews who saw Jesus raise Lazarus from the grave
began to believe in him, but some went directly to the chief priest
Caiaphas to tell him what they had seen. The entire passage reads as
follows:

"Now many of the Jews who had come to Mary and seen
what he had done began to believe in him. But some of them
went to the Pharisees and told them what Jesus had done. So
the chief priests and the Pharisees convened the Sanhedrin

and said, "What are we going to do? This man is performing many signs. If we leave him alone, all will believe in him, and the Romans will come and take away both our land and our nation. <u>But one of them, Caiaphas, who was high priest that year, said to them, "You know nothing, nor do you consider that it is better for you that one man should die instead of the people, so that the whole nation shall not perish.</u> So from that day on they planned to kill him."[147]

As the passage in John 11:49-51 shows, the same kind of thought process that Hitler used to justify the killing of Jews as a means of saving humanity was also used by the chief priest Caiaphas to convince himself that the killing of Jesus would protect the Jewish nation.

If nothing else, the New Testament makes very clear that Caiaphas and the Pharisees made their living as the experts in the laws of Moses. They in fact got very wealthy in their Pharisaic positions. Caiaphas got very nervous when the Pharisees told him how Jesus was building a large group of followers with a message that was diametrically opposite to what the Pharisees were pushing. Jesus was teaching the laws of consciousness (God) and telling people that it was okay to not follow the laws of Moses to the letter, as the Pharisees commanded them to do, so long as not following them to the letter did not violate the laws of God. The best delineation of the laws of God at that time were the Ten Commandments., which Jesus broke down further to his two greatest commandments to love God with all one's strength, soul and mind and to love each other as we love ourselves.

The Pharisees knew that if Jesus' message caught on, they would be out of business as the experts and enforcers of the hundreds of Mosaic laws. As the Pharisee-in-Chief, Caiaphas could not let that probability stand. Based upon what was told to Caiaphas by the Pharisees, a Sanhedrin was convened where the Pharisees made the case that if Jesus was left alone to do as he has been doing, then the jig would be up for them. They argued that the Romans would come and take away both their land and nation. What they really meant was that the back office deal done behind closed doors with Rome whereby they would police their own people if Rome left them alone to do as they please would be off the table and they would be under their thumb of Rome the same way their own people were under its thumb. It was Caiaphas' job as their leader to make sure that didn't happen. So, the decision was made to have Jesus arrested so that they could arrange for his death after a rigged trial. That was Caiaphas' way of 'saving the nation' just as it was Hitler's way of 'saving humanity' by rounding up the Social Democrats and Jews and putting them in death camps. Of course, it goes without saying that 'saving the nation' and 'saving humanity' were politically correct code words that allowed everyone involved to feel righteous and good about themselves while killing innocents.

Like Hitler, Caiaphas was a master illusionist and therefore no one questioned the insanity of his response when he told the Pharisees who came to him warning about Jesus, "Ye know nothing at all, nor consider that it is expedient for us, that one man [Jesus] should die for the people, and that the whole nation perish not."[148] A more logical person may have viewed Caiaphas' reaction as extreme and asked him if other, less severe avenues could be pursued other than the demonization and destruction of the man himself. However, what I have learned through research and personal experience is that logic has no place in an authoritarian mind that holds certain beliefs and has tied its entire existence to those beliefs. Why would such a mind entertain alternate viewpoints if the alternate viewpoints are in opposition? Why would Hitler entertain the fact that Social Democrats were not the sub-human threats to humanity he was convinced they were when in order to hold that view, he would have had to give up all the hate, anger and feelings of revenge his seventeen-year-old mind had created and to which his power and control was linked? Why would Caiaphas entertain the fact that Jesus' message was attracting so many crowds when that message would spell the end of Mosaic law, upon which Caiaphas and the Pharisees had built their temple empire of power and wealth? The simple answer is he would not entertain it when he could use that wealth and power to kill the messenger and thereby silence the message.

When Caiaphas heard about Jesus, his immediate reaction was to find a way to get rid of him. Not once did he float the idea of meeting with Jesus to talk to him or try to understand what it was he was teaching that was having such a powerful impact on the community. He didn't have to when he had the power to just get rid of him. And it was not only Jesus he planned on getting rid of. John 12:10-11 says that the chief priests plotted to kill Lazarus too because many people were becoming followers of Jesus because of him. That is how these powerful illusionists operate. They don't only get rid of the troublemaker(s) in their eyes. They get rid of all the people surrounding the troublemaker who could potentially cause them trouble. Human life means absolutely nothing to them when they perceive their power is threatened.[149]

Instead of questioning Caiaphas about what he meant by saying he was 'saving the nation' by killing Jesus, all his little lap dogs concurred and went along with his plan to kill an innocent man. They developed a calculated strategy to go out and purposefully get Jesus to say or do something he shouldn't do or say in order to get him accused of a death penalty crime. The four gospels of Jesus in the New Testament are rife with examples of the Pharisees trying to do just that.

One of the crimes they tried to set him up with was blasphemy.

They would follow him around and ask him questions that they felt sure they could slip him up with so they could arrest him. [See Matthew 22:15-22 where they tried to entrap him in speech by getting him to say that people should not pay their taxes. Also see Mark 10:1-2 where it says, "The Pharisees approached him and asked, 'Is it lawful for a husband to divorce his wife?' They were testing him."]

I think it was because of their unrelenting efforts to entrap him in speech that Jesus began conveying his message in parables, allegories and stories because fictional stories and parables do not constitute blasphemy, yet they are effective in relaying important truths. As I show in chapter seven, I believe Jesus had an advantage of which the Pharisees stalking him were unaware. He had studied the law during what has been called his 'lost years.' He knew some of the Pharisees who stalked him because he went to school with them. The Bible even says that he ate dinner with the Pharisees.[150] He knew them and they knew him. He was on friendly terms with at least some of them if he had dinner with them. It would therefore not be surprising if one or more of them heard about Caiaphas' plan to have him arrested and warned him so he could protect himself.

It was never a matter of God sending his only son to die for our sins. It was always about protecting the self-interests of a cruel, manipulative power broker who felt threatened. Rationalizations come in very handy for people like Caiaphas because if they were upfront about their motives, they would be seen for the murderers, slanderers and monsters they really are. And so Caiaphas came up with one of the best rationalizations of all time for justifying the destruction of a person's reputation, livelihood and life in a battle to gain or retain power that cannot otherwise be gained on the merits. It is called the 'greater good' rationalization.

Both Caiaphas and Hitler used the greater good rationalization to dispose of people they didn't like. Neither man had God's laws, or man-made laws for that matter, to back them up in their killing of innocent people. They had to resort to lies and the changing of laws to get convictions and death. However, they were both very quick to use God as their shield. It was the same shield Samuel used against Saul when Saul used his own judgment to make a decision in the heat of battle, while disregarding the human destruction that Samuel had ordered him to commit.

These masters of illusion will always use righteous rationalizations for their bad actions and orders. Luckily for them, God is always at hand. It is good to always keep in mind that evil always hides behind what we label as righteousness. Otherwise, evil would not exist because we would see it for what it is, both in ourselves and in other people.

Motive

If we are to ever fully understand why any person thinks or acts in a certain way, we must understand their motive. A motive is defined as an idea, belief or emotion that impels a person to act in accordance with that state of mind.[151] Jesus said all evil behavior arises out of the motives we have for doing what we do, telling his disciples that evil thoughts, murder, adultery, unchastity, theft and lies all arise out of the mind and not from any external factors like peer pressure, authority, laws or ideology.[152] Those external factors may provide us with the incentive we need to do something, but the underlying motive is always the thoughts we have that impel us to act in accordance with those thoughts.

One of the lessons of the allegory of Adam and Eve is that sin lies in our motive for doing what we do. Woman knows it is against the rules/law of the Garden to eat the fruit, but her rationalization that the law was put in place to keep her from having the same knowledge as God gives her the leeway (gray area) she needs in order to take a bite. Her motive for eating the fruit is wanting to have the same knowledge as God. If her motive for eating the fruit had never come into existence, her thoughts would have remained in alignment with the law. The snake brought her motive/incentive into existence and to that extent, the serpent represents the human ego consciousness that creates the incentive in this world to act in accordance with one's own self-interests without considering how that incentive may negatively impact someone else.

We should always keep in mind that Adam and Eve, who are referred to simply as Man and Woman throughout the story, are literary devices the Bible writers use to represent the mental processes all human beings use to create and justify bad behavior. These two characters give us insight into the fatal mental processes to which we can all fall victim and that keep us from realizing the purpose and destiny for our lives. Woman's motive in eating the fruit is to have the same knowledge as God so she can usurp God's authority as the Creator of the Garden and implement rules more conducive to getting what she wants, and Adam's motive in following her behavior is to protect his own physical self-interests. By the time God shows up, Adam and Eve are on top of the world eating all the fruit they want without guilt or regret under the now internalized assumption that they are the ones making all the rules. As far as they are concerned, the Garden is just as God left it. Their clothes have become as natural as their nakedness once was. Every thought they previously held with a consciousness of truth has long since been manipulated and rationalized out of existence to conform to an ego that serves its own self-interests.

The internal disorder they create within their minds after

reworking universal laws in their own favor reflect back on their external environment and paradise soon gives way to a disordered existence where they are creating their own rules in a world where personal survival, not communal fulfillment, becomes the goal. This is allegorically represented when God kicks them out of the Garden and they are forever prevented from having the same kind of peace, joy and tranquility they had in the Garden.

We will never discover our individual destinies while operating within internal and external structures that nurture a consciousness of illusion created by the same kinds of rationalizations and lies that Eve used to eat the fruit without guilt. Through their irrational thinking process, Eve and Adam create an endless loop where they will always be able to come up with arguments to justify their wrong behavior. With self-satisfaction as the only motive for what we do, there is no limit to the excuses we are capable of creating to justify our actions.

Morality and ethics become very complicated when people create their own playbooks for what is and is not acceptable in satisfying their own personal agendas. As more and more victims are created by the harm this egoistic morality engenders, more and more laws are passed in a futile effort to stop the chaos.

Sin was never about what we do. It has always been about the motive for doing what we do. When we organized society so that the stronger egos would rise to the top of the pyramid as they did in the animal kingdom, we built sin and evil into the system and into ourselves. We are not born in sin. We learn how to sin in order to survive financially and otherwise in a society that is structured largely on the animal consciousness of our past. This is not the traditional view of religion, but it is the good news of the Bible because anything learned can be unlearned.

Questioning ourselves and our motives for why we are doing

what we are doing is the only way any of us ever get to the truth so that we can initiate change. Man and Woman have three opportunities to set the record straight and get back on track with why they were put in the Garden, but instead they choose to lie and make excuses for what they did.

Religious leaders who say we are in a constant battle with Satan who they euphemistically refer to as the enemy, as if there is a spirit flying around putting bad thoughts in our heads and making us do what we do not want to do, are providing us with the biggest self-delusion of all. Unfortunately, an entire doctrine has been built on it and sold to people just like Adam and Eve who want to continue doing what they do but not get blamed for it.

In Matthew 7:21-23, Jesus says, "Not everyone who says to me, "Lord, Lord,' will enter the kingdom of heaven, but only the one who does the will of my Father in heaven. Many will say to me on that day, 'Lord, Lord, did we not prophesy in your name? Did we not drive out demons in your name? Did we not do mighty deeds in your name? Then I will declare to them solemnly, 'I never knew you. Depart from me, you evildoers." Jesus is addressing here the kind of morality that looks outward and tells us we are bad people if we do certain things. It is an "in the eye of the beholder" method of separating us by what we do rather than how we think. When one looks outward, one looks at groups of people. When one looks inward, one can only look at oneself. Jesus knew that the only way we can make a substantive change on the macro – organizational and societal level – is by fixing thoughts at the core level; one mind at a time.

We cannot always know if our motives for doing what we do are completely pure or if the actions we take are correct, but we are obligated, as the energy of consciousness, to make an effort to align our energetic thoughts with the laws of consciousness as much as possible, so that our actions are always aligned as well. Proverbs 16:25 says: "Sometimes a way seems right, but the end of it leads to death." We have all made mistakes in judgment and done things that we have regretted later; hence the saying 'we learn from our mistakes'. The key to living a happy and fulfilled life is to lessen those mistakes now, so that we do not have regrets later. There are two simple questions we can ask ourselves before taking any action that will help us do just that: Is what I am about to do going to harm myself (in terms of my own consciousness of reality and illusion)? Is what I am about to do going to harm anyone else? It takes nothing less than constant, daily vigilance in seeking out what our true motives are in doing what we do so that we always take the

right action.

Chapter 7
The Targeting of Jesus

I Come Not to Destroy the Law

It is my opinion that there is a direct line from the mobbing that resulted in the conviction and ordered execution of Jesus to the National Socialist German Workers Party doctrine that resulted in the holocaust. The patterns of corruption used by the Pharisaic leadership against Jesus were the same patterns of corruption Hitler used to seize power and exert control over the people of Germany and the nations he invaded. Hitler loved the hierarchical structure because a hierarchy has always been the preferred structure in which corrupt people like to operate. Power can coalesce at the top where the dictator/tyrant/CEO/Chief Priest/delegation can direct all their hand-picked minions. They can appoint all their incompetent cronies to serve as gatekeepers at each level of the pyramid, dispense with the people who do not go along with the agenda, spread blame downward and reward allies with all the carrots and perks at their disposal.

In the case of Jesus, he definitely did not go along with the agenda. We all know Jesus was a rabbi and teacher, but why has no one ever asked how he became a rabbi? He could not just announce himself as one and make it so. Like all the other Pharisees and Sadduccees of his day, he would have had to have gone to school to study Mosaic law. And indeed he did. In the scriptures that were banned by the hierarchy of the Church, it says:

"Jesus conceals his miracles, 2 studies the law, 3 and is baptized. NOW from this time Jesus began to conceal his miracles and secret works, 2 And gave himself to the study of the law, till he arrived to the end of his thirtieth year." [See The First Gospel of the Infancy of Jesus Christ.[153]

To me, the fact that Jesus was a rabbi who studied the law adds another whole new layer of pain to his story. He was not an outsider. He dined with the Pharisees and knew them all intimately after having worked and gone to school with many of them. It wasn't strangers who railroaded, convicted and spit on him with such rancor and hate. It was colleagues and friends. It must have taken the energy of every cell in his body to then ask God to forgive them while on the cross they built for him.

We never expect anyone to turn on us with such vengeance for saying what we believe, but when it is colleagues and trusted friends who do it, the trauma and pain of it never goes away. That is why bullying and mobbing causes such trauma to its victims – because it is schoolmates, colleagues and people you considered friends who participate in it.

Throughout the first four books of the New Testament there are numerous incidents where the Pharisees are in the presence of Jesus just waiting for him to say something that would justify his arrest under the hundreds of Mosaic laws in place. Those laws covered all aspects of a Jew's life; thereby giving the corrupt Pharisees the means to entrap anyone. It is the same strategy Hitler used when he passed all-encompassing laws like that of Protective Custody; whereby the State had the power to imprison people without judicial proceedings. Within the body of a typical Order for Protective Custody was the sentence, "You are taken into protective custody in the interest of public security and order." This sentence basically gave the SS police the power to arrest anyone under the justification that their actions and/or speech was a threat to public security and order.[154]

Jesus said in Matthew 5:17, "Think not that I am come to destroy the law, or the prophets: I am not come to destroy, but to fulfill." I believe that with this one sentence, Jesus made himself a target of the Pharisees. With this one sentence. Jesus showed himself to be a whistle blower telling the truth. As I pointed out in the previous chapter, the Pharisees had made themselves the subject matter experts and enforcers of Mosaic laws that covered every aspect of a Jew's life. They had total control over the community with those laws, but those laws were not the laws Jesus was interested in. In fact, he reminded his disciples on multiple occasions that they were the controllers of their own lives and therefore could decide for themselves when to fast, what to eat, how to pray and so forth. The laws Jesus was fulfilling were the ten laws that Moses brought down the mountain. However, if each person was to maintain order and peace within the community by following those ten laws, what need would they have for their Pharisaic leaders? It would mean the illusion would be revealed for what it is — an elaborate scheme for Pharisaic-like leaders to get rich by going to law school to become experts in the hundreds and thousands of laws that are used to control their populations. Jesus says as much in his denunciation of the Pharisees in Matthew, Chapter 23:

> "For they preach but they do not practice [hypocrites]. They tie up heavy burdens and lay them on people's shoulders, but they will not lift a finger to move them. [Because it serves their greedy self-interests] All their works are performed to be seen. [Appearances] They love places of

honor at banquets, seats of honor in synagogues, greetings in marketplaces, and the salutation 'Rabbi.'"

Replace the last word 'Rabbi' in the verse above with judge, senator, president, CEO, manager, director, professor, doctor, pastor, prime minister, and all the political and other hypocrites in leadership positions who think it is fine and good to make others follow the rules and laws they come up with but to which they themselves are exempt and you will get the picture Jesus was painting for us.

As you can imagine, the Pharisees despised Jesus for calling out their pyramid scheme of power; so, like most whistle blowers, the wheels were set in motion to destroy Jesus one way or another so that the truth would never get out and the power held by the Pharisees over the Jewish community would forever be secured.

Jesus' crucifixion began long before he was nailed to the cross. He was the target of a mobbing, just as the Jews in Germany were mobbed. Bullying and mobbing is animal-like behavior arising out of the group think of a gang led by an authoritarian leader. It is a malicious gang strategy used to force someone from the workplace (or in the case of Jews in Nazi Germany, from society at large) by getting their colleagues/neighbors/friends to isolate, exclude, intimidate, discredit, degrade and lie about them. It is behavior found in the animal kingdom when members of the same species collectively attack or harass a predator or outsider in the group. The motive for this behavior when animals do it is usually to protect the cohesiveness of the group. It is the same with people who employ it. They want to protect the cohesiveness of the gang by getting rid of any predators they perceive as a threat.

In the upside-down world of the gang, all truth tellers who put the gang at risk are considered the predators and labeled as troublemakers, non-team players, liars and worse. Jesus was called crazy when he came right out and asked the Pharisees why they were trying to kill him, which is exactly what they were trying to do.[155] A corrupt mob can never handle the truth and will always resort to name calling and personal attacks when faced with it by the target of their abuse. This is the reason many whistle-blowers are targeted by the mob. Their truth telling exposes the wrongdoing of one or more of the gang members and thereby puts the entire gang at risk. The gang comes together to protect the member, knowing the same will be done for them if they should find themselves in a similar situation. Most humans have evolved out of this kind of behavior because we have the ability to reason and observe the harm that always results to the target of the abusive behavior.

However, there are two forces alive and well in the workplace that provide the breeding ground for this type of ganging up behavior against a target – what I have been referring to as mobbing: (1) the hierarchical structure of authority found in most organizations and (2) the pressure human beings feel to conform their thinking to the authoritarian figures who serve as their gatekeepers at each level of the organizational structures. This conformance in thinking is also commonly referred to as group-think.

Jesus was bullied and mobbed out of his job as a rabbi and teacher by the religious clergy of his day known as the Pharisees. They wanted Jesus out of the way because he was upsetting the status quo they set up which was providing them with great status and financial rewards. At first, they tried to undermine him in front of the crowds he was attracting. When that didn't work for them and the people loved Jesus all the more for the genius of his handling of them, the Pharisees turned to Judas who was willing to betray his friend and teacher for money.

The Pharisees responsible for killing Jesus held psychopathic states of mind that Jesus gives us a glimpse into with his parable of the tenant farmers found in Mark 12 and Luke 20. Jesus' *Parable of the Tenants*[156] is an illustration of how an animal consciousness of survival has no regard for anyone or anything except its own self-preservation. Similar to a wild dog, its evolution of mind has stopped at physical protection and it will demolish any person or thing that threatens its interests. In the parable, a man goes on a journey and leaves his vineyard to several tenant farmers while he is away. At the agreed upon time, he sends a servant to collect the rent from the farmers but the farmers beat him and send him away empty-handed. The man then sends another servant, who they beat even more severely and treat far more shamefully. The man sends yet another servant and another servant who the farmers alternately beat and/or kill. Last of all, he sends his own son who he loves very much to collect the money, reasoning that the farmers will certainly respect him enough to pay what they owe. When the son arrives to collect the rent, he too is killed under the false assumption that the son's inheritance will be theirs now that the man has no son.

As usual, when Jesus told the parable of the tenant farmers Pharisee spies were in the crowd listening to his every word in order to arrest him. Mark 12:12 says that after Jesus told the parable, they [the Pharisees] were going to arrest him because they knew the parable was addressed to them, but they feared the crowd and left. [I should also mention that power abusers hate the truth; particularly when the truth reveals the corruption they try so hard to hide.]

As human beings who are evolving, most of us have a hard time understanding the mindset of a power abuser. As a human being living among other human beings, we understand the logic of taking the interests of other people into account, along with our own, when making decisions. That is the whole purpose of having a set of rules and values in place. They get us all on the same page as to how we should behave and what we can expect from others in terms of behavior.

Rules and values mean nothing to power abusers other than how they can be manipulated to work in their favor. The parable of the tenant farmers clearly shows us why the appeasement of Hitler before the war failed. Appeasement never works because power abusers can never be appeased. They will use the appeasement process to take more and more and more. Then once the appeaser realizes there will never be an end point and gives up, the power abuser just continues on with the agenda he/she had in mind in the first place.

In the case of a mobbing, the agenda is always to eliminate the human target(s). Because of the relentlessness of the attack mounted against them, most all targets are eventually worn down by all the negative stress they experience and usually lash out in some way. Their actions are then used against them by the perpetrators as a means for banishing them from the workplace. In the case of Jesus, the numerous attempts by the Pharisees to trick him into saying something blasphemous so they could arrest him all failed. He gave them the chance they were waiting for with his outburst in the temple where he threw over the tables of the money changers. I believe that act served as a release for all of Jesus' negative stress and it was then used as the reason for his arrest. Judas provided them with the opportune time for arresting Jesus when there were no crowds around him to get in the way.

The negative stress caused by bullying and mobbing also causes victims to make desperate and ill-thought-out choices in desperate attempts to save themselves, their careers and their livelihoods. In my book, *The Mobbing of Jesus Christ*, I write in detail about how and why Jesus made a very fateful choice in using pagan resurrection myths as a blueprint for giving the Pharisees the sign they kept asking him for to prove that he was the Messiah. As I talk about in the next chapter of this book, that choice allowed the chief priests to turn the tables on him and his message because it was not grounded in truth. It continues to be used against him to the current day as proof that he was a mythological figure rather than a real person.

The ability of power abusers to turn the tables on us when we use lies and/or deception of any kind to fortress an agenda or position is something that all people should be made aware. Lies and deception belong in the realm of illusion. Even though you may think you are fortifying your position by using them, the masters of illusion can always use them against you because they have a power advantage. They are the ones who change legacies and rewrite history. The innocent person in an interrogation room who lies (confesses) in an attempt to alleviate the pressure exerted upon them, will always lose. The liar with more power and control will ALWAYS win. Even though it appears like telling the truth in a high-pressure situation is a losing battle, never fall into the trap. Truth and reality will protect you, your soul, your legacy and your eternal consciousness in the long-term even if suffering is inevitable in the short-term.

It is a fact that all victims of a mobbing will suffer injury. The perpetrators purposely go after a person's core consciousness in order to make them believe they are worthless and make everyone else think they are the cause of the problem, rather than placing blame where it belongs - on the perpetrator(s) of the mobbing who are abusing their power. Since people want to side with the winner, they join in the campaign of degradation and destruction. In the case of Jesus, he rode into Jerusalem for the Passover to crowds calling him the Messiah and a few days later, that same crowd was yelling for his execution at the urging of the elders and chief priests. When a target is up against a powerful leader with influence, their fate is pretty well sealed. These leaders surround themselves with loyal followers who carry out their orders in exchange for perks like money, promotions, extra vacation time, handsome salaries and bonuses, good evaluations and all the other carrots the leader has at his disposal. Morals can quickly go by the wayside when a person's financial livelihood is at risk.

Bullies are nothing other than power abusers and they come in all varieties: individuals, pairs, management teams and entire organizations and governments. The stronger their influence, the fewer options a target has. One of the saddest interviews I ever watched was of a holocaust survivor who said she kept asking herself when America would come to her rescue while she waited in a concentration camp. I just recently read this same refrain coming from a woman in a refugee camp in the Middle East, wondering why all the world has abandoned them. Targets wait and wait and wait for someone to come to their rescue and the majority of them wait forever because there is no one to fill that role. They are completely disposable and once gone, the power abusing organizations go on as if nothing ever happened while the targets either commit suicide or spend the rest of their lives trying to recover from the assault.

Jesus was hounded, persecuted and harassed by the Pharisees in their attempts to arrest him. In fact, it is startling how similar the tactics used by supposed 'holy' men against Jesus were identical to the tactics used by Hitler against the Jews, Social Democrats, disabled, dissidents, Christians, Freemasons and a host of other groups in Nazi-occupied Germany.

Just as Hitler used a step-by-step process to demonize, isolate and eventually exterminate the class of human beings he viewed as sub-human, under the false justification that he was saving humanity by so doing, Caiaphas and the Pharisees used a mirror process to demonize, isolate and eventually eradicate Jesus from the community under the false justification they were saving the nation by doing so.

I wrote an entire book on how the mobbing against Jesus was carried out. Below is just a synopsis of the mobbing to give you, the reader, a sense of how it mirrored all mobbings; including the one orchestrated by Hitler against the Jews in Nazi Germany.

DIAGRAM OF A MOBBING

I. The Bullying Against Jesus Begins.

The power abusing Pharisees felt threatened by Jesus. When predatory power abusers feel threatened, they attack the perceived threat with the intent of eventually eliminating them. The chief priest Caiaphas felt so threatened that he ordered the arrest and execution of Jesus. [John 11:49-51]

a. Character Assassination

Jesus made a mute person speak and the crowds were amazed, saying, "Nothing like this has ever been seen in Israel. But the Pharisees said, "He drives demons out by the prince of demons." [Matthew 9:32-34]

They also call him a glutton and drunkard. In Matthew 11:18-19, Jesus says, "For John came neither eating nor drinking, and they said, 'He is possessed by a demon.' The Son of Man came eating and drinking and they said, 'Look, he is a glutton and a drunkard, a friend of tax collectors and sinners." Additionally, they call him crazy when he asks them why they are trying to kill him, which is exactly what they were trying to do. [See Luke 7:17-20]

II. The Conspiracy Against Jesus (Yes, Virginia, there are conspiracies)

> "Then the chief priests and the elders of the people assembled in the palace of the high priest and they consulted together to arrest Jesus by treachery and put him to death."
> [Matthew 26:1-5]

When word got back to Caiaphas and the Council that Jesus was gaining in popularity and could threaten their power base, they leaped into action to plot his demise behind the closed doors of the palace of the high priest. Power abusers at the top of the hierarchy will always seek out the support of their buddies in management and HR to back them up in their lies and character assassination against the target. They want to protect their managerial power base against the 'troublemakers' (code word for employees and whistle blowers who dare to speak up about mismanagement and wrongdoing). Together, they work behind the scenes to plot the best ways for terminating the person they have labeled as a problem; just as Hitler labeled the Jews a problem requiring the Final Solution.

III. Use of Provocateurs/Spies

> "They [the Pharisees] watched him closely and sent agents pretending to be righteous who were to trap him in speech, in order to hand him over to the authority and power of the governor." [Luke 20:20]

The Pharisee spies served the same function as the blockleiter in Nazi Germany who spied and reported on the activities of their neighbors.

IV. The Betrayal by Judas.

> "Then Judas Iscariat went to the chief priests and said,

"What are you willing to give me if I hand him over to you?" They paid him thirty pieces of silver and from that on he looked for an opportunity to hand him over." [Matthew 26:14-16]

Judas sold out Jesus for 30 pieces of silver. In the modern workplace, employees routinely sell out their target colleagues for the price of keeping their job, or as protection from becoming targets themselves. It was this dynamic that made the Blockleiter in Nazi Germany so successful in turning in their neighbors and friends.

Since I have previously discussed how motive is such an integral factor in our behavior and the actions we choose to take, I think it is important to delve a little bit into what the motive may have been for Judas to betray his leader, mentor and friend. Matthew 26:6-13 and Mark 14:3-9 both describe an incident that took place the day before Jesus entered Jerusalem for the last time before the Passover. While Jesus was having dinner at the home of Lazarus, Mary anointed his feet with a very costly perfumed oil. The disciples got very annoyed by this because they believed the oil could have been sold to help with their expenses. In the verse following both passages it says that Judas Iscariot went to the chief priests asking how much he could get paid for handing over Jesus. [See Matthew 26:14 and Mark:10-11].

Judas was the treasurer for the group. The perceived waste of money with the oil probably got him very angry and we all have done and said things we regret in fits of anger. Also, while in a state of anger, we usually don't stop to think about the unintended consequences of our words or actions. It appears to me that Judas' decision to go to the chief priests may have been a spur of the moment type thing taken in the heat of anger. He was not in a position in the hierarchy to have known that the chief priest, Caiaphas, had ordered the execution of Jesus. The shock of what he did after witnessing the crucifixion, not to mention the alienation he would have had to endure from the other disciples, is what I believe prompted him to commit suicide after throwing the Pharisee's payment back at them. Unlike the Pharisees, Judas was a decent man who still had the ability to feel guilt and shame. To me, his suicide indicates he was very sorry for the choice he made in the heat of the moment; having been left with no means to make things right or apologize to the human being he harmed through his action. Caiaphas and his Pharisee minions – the people who actually committed the crime of killing Jesus – never felt an ounce of guilt or shame because it was their intent to kill Jesus to save themselves, their power and wealth; yet they are the ones who have gotten off pretty much scot-free. Unfortunately, that is the way it usually works and that is why powerfully corrupt people like Samuel and Caiaphas love to use the strategies of the mob for picking off their perceived enemies. Hitler wasn't so lucky due to the fact that he had what turned out to be a more powerful target in the form of the Allied invaders.

V. Disciples' Abandonment of Jesus.

> "And immediately a cock crowed. Then Peter remembered the word that Jesus had spoken: "Before the cock crows you will deny me three times." He went out and began to weep bitterly." [Matthew 26:75]

Bystanders in bullying and mobbing incidents will cooperate in isolating, ignoring, excluding and gossiping about the target and then later on deny that they ever played any part in the mobbing. Peter, of course, is the disciple we all hear about in denying Jesus, but what about the other 10 disciples? They all slept in the garden of Gethsemane when Jesus needed them most and then fled when the soldiers came to arrest him. None of them ever showed up at the trial to testify on Jesus' behalf, nor were they at the cross to ease him through his suffering. They acted cowardly, as do all workplace colleagues who see a target crying and falling apart at the seams and yet fail to do or say anything to support him/her.

VI. Jesus' Agony in the Garden.

"Then he [Jesus] said to them, "My soul is sorrowful even to death. Remain here and keep watch with me." He advanced a little and fell prostrate in prayer, saying "My Father. If it is possible, let this cup pass from me; yet not as I will, but as you will." When he returned to his disciples, he found them asleep. [Matthew 26: 36-46]

Unless you have been a victim yourself, you cannot comprehend how people in a workplace would intentionally set out to gaslight and destroy the career of someone they work with. Churches should make this the cornerstone of their teachings. It was no coincidence that Jesus was bullied and mobbed. He was dealing with the face of evil in the form of the Pharisees – people who thought they were good people just because they convinced themselves they were. They did good things, but that does not make someone good. It never will. It was people who think it's what they do and not who they are who Jesus was addressing when he said they would come to him in the kingdom saying, "Lord, Lord, did we not prophesy in your name? Did we not drive out demons in your name? Did we not do mighty deeds in your name?" Jesus said he would then declare to them solemnly, "I never knew you." [Matthew 7:22]

VII. The Arrest of Jesus.

"At that hour Jesus said to the crowds, "Have you come out as against a robber, with swords and clubs to seize me? Day after day I sat teaching in the temple area, yet you did not arrest me ... Then all the disciples left him and fled." [Matthew 26:55-56]

Jesus was arrested in an empty garden in the dark of night when there were multiple occasions to arrest him in daylight while he was in the temple. In modern-day workplaces, a person who is terminated is escorted out of the building with their box so that they do not talk to anyone and no one talks to them. They could have arrested Jesus at any time, but instead they waited until nightfall when he was alone with his disciples and away from the crowds who followed him wherever he went.

Until someone has been objectified and experienced the humiliation of being treated like a criminal for doing the right thing, they will never fully understand how horrible and cruel these bullying and mobbing behaviors are. Totalitarian regimes are set up so that the majority of the population is put on the lower rung of the hierarchy and in a position to be objectified by those in power. Once a person or group is turned into an object through propaganda, stereotyping, character assassination and other tactics used by corrupt people in power (like the Caiaphas and the Council), it can open the door to unimaginable abuse. The only way to prevent such a fate is for individuals to stand up and speak out against injustice and cruelty whenever and wherever they see it occurring to someone or some group. This was Jesus' message in a nutshell. Spirit (God) within all of us makes us all equal members of the human race. Our pay scale, gender, race, sexual orientation or job title should not be taken into account when it comes to treating people with the respect and dignity we all deserve as eternal beings of consciousness inhabiting an ephemeral physical body on a physical plane.

VIII. The Mob Mentality Takes Over.

"The chief priests and the elders persuaded the crowds to ask for Barabbas but to destroy Jesus. ...Pilate offered the crowd the choice of saving Barabbas, a notorious criminal, and Jesus. "Which one do you want me to release to you, Barabbas or Jesus?" For he knew it was out of envy that they had handed him over. .. They all said, "Let him [Jesus] be crucified!" But he said, "Why? What evil has he done?" They only shouted the louder, "Let him be crucified." [Matthew 26:18-23]

And then there is this passage from the gospels the Church has deemed are heretical.

"16 The Jews say to Pilate, Our law command us not to put any one to death. We desire that he may be crucified, because he deserves the death of the cross.18 But when the governor looked upon the people that were present and the Jews, <u>he saw many of the Jews in tears, and said to the chief priests of the Jews, All the people do not desire his death.</u> 19 The elders of the Jews answered to Pilate, We and all the people came hither for this very purpose, that he should die. 20 Pilate saith to them, Why should he die? 21 They said to him, Because he declares himself to be the Son of God and a King.[157]

Under Jewish law, execution was not allowed. The cowards needed Pilate to do their dirty work; so they told Pilate lies to get him to kill Jesus. Jesus purposely never referred to himself as the Son of God, as the Pharisees claimed; choosing instead to call himself the Son of Man. Also, the Pharisees claimed that Jesus wanted to make himself king; however, it wasn't Jesus who wanted to be king. It was the crowds who listened to him wanting to make him a king. It says in John 6:15, "Since Jesus knew that they [the crowds] were going to come and carry him off to make him king, he withdrew again to the mountain alone."

The elders and chief priests were in fact pathological liars who told lie after lie in order to get Jesus convicted. Jesus never had a chance against such power brokers who stacked the deck against him.

The passage above makes clear that the Jewish people themselves did not want Jesus to die. If the institution of the church had given a hearing to all the gospels, and not just the letters of Paul that make up most of the New Testament, this fact would have been made clear and all the anti-Semitic haters that followed over the years would not have been given a safe haven for their lies and cruelty. Also, 'Saint Paul' would have been exposed as the originator of this lie and his letters and doctrine would have been thrown in the trash bin of history for the propaganda they are. In 1 Thessalonians 2:14-15, the unsaintly Paul says,

> "For you, brothers, have become imitators of the churches of God that are in Judea in Christ Jesus. For you suffer the same things from your compatriots as they did from the Jews, who killed both the Lord Jesus and the prophets and persecuted us. They do not please God, and are opposed to everyone."

It was Paul who first floated the idea that the Jews killed Jesus, in direct contradiction to his doctrine that Jesus came in human form to die for the forgiveness of sins. He set the foundation for Hitler and all the other Anti-Semites who came before and after him and gave them safe haven in the Christian churches that focus on his false doctrine.

Chapter 8
Sin That Cannot Be Forgiven
According to Jesus

Actions like the conscious killing of innocent people cannot be committed by a human mind that is grounded in truth; which is why bad actions are usually hidden behind righteous rationalizations. Hitler is an example. In many of his speeches, he passionately conveyed that he was saving humanity by ridding the world of 'the Jew.' The chief priest, Caiaphas, claimed he was saving the nation by ridding the world of Jesus. How many wars have been justified under the banner of ridding the world of tyranny and protecting freedom?

Truth is the antidote to these kinds of false rationalizations and it has been since the time the allegory of Adam and Eve was written, when the character of God walking through the Garden tries to cut through Man and Woman's justifications and lies by asking them questions. They choose their lies over truth and pass blame around with Adam blaming Eve and Eve blaming the snake. It made it impossible for them to look at themselves truthfully, so that they could give truthful answers.

The only way to acquire a spirit of truth is to eradicate the falsehoods we tell ourselves to get our thinking to conform to 'other than' truth. Most of us have been living with 'other than' truth for so long that we do not even know our assumptions are false. I was recently reading an article about employers who will not hire someone who is unemployed reasoning that if they were a good employee they would have never lost their job in the first place.[158] This is a totally irrational assumption in a society where employers are routinely cutting the size of their work forces simply to avoid paying benefits, sending jobs overseas, laying people off and then hiring contractors and part-time employees to replace them.

Jesus makes clear in the Book of John that the holy spirit is not a third entity that enters your body at the calling of his name. He tells his disciples in John 14:15-20 that the advocate he is sending them is "the Spirit of Truth, which the world cannot accept because it neither sees nor knows it. But you know it, because it remains with you and will be in you" and when he comes, "the Spirit of truth will guide you to all truth." [John 13:16]

If the eradication of falsehoods is the spirit of truth, then logic is the language of truth. When I took computer programming courses, all the programs I wrote were logical progressions of if-then statements. If 'a' happens, then 'b', but if not 'a' then 'c'. There is no room for doubt. It either happens or it doesn't.

I can't help but think that as conscious, energetic beings with the ability to choose, there must be some kind of programming involved with the creation of human consciousness. If we choose one thing, something happens. If we choose another, something else happens. If-then. Cause and effect. In that sense, our consciousness is very similar to a computer's program because computers work much like human beings in their information-processing capabilities. If they follow one set of instructions, then there is a certain result. However, if they follow another set of instructions, there is a different result. Both computers and individual human beings can only act on the information that is given. If that information is limited, the processing results are limited and the machine is reduced in its capabilities to produce quality output. Or if that information is false, then the results are false.

This limited processing capability in the individual human mind based on limited and false information is clearly on display in heavily indoctrinated and propagandized environments. It causes the phenomenon that William Shirer described in *The Rise and Fall of the Third Reich* when he said that he would be met with stares of incredulity and shocks of silence whenever he would offer a differing viewpoint to what a stranger in a restaurant or cafe voiced after their mind had become warped by Hitler's and Goebbels' propaganda.

Interestingly enough, Jesus was met with the same shocks of silence from the Pharisees when he would combat their irrationality with logic. Matthew 22:41-45 tells of an encounter between Jesus and a group of Pharisees where Jesus asks them, "What do you think of the Messiah? Whose son is he?" In accordance with their doctrine, the Pharisees answer, "David's." Jesus then quotes Psalm 110:1 to them as follows, "The Lord says to my lord; "Sit at my right hand, while I make your enemies your footstool," and asks them, "If David calls him 'lord,' how can he be his son?" The passage finishes by saying that the group then fell silent and from that day on, did not dare ask Jesus any questions.

To put it in terms of programming language, Shirer and Jesus were both unable to use logic and truth to make contact with the minds of the average German citizen and Pharisee, respectively, because both groups had reached what is called in computer programming their END STATEMENT. In such a mind, the programming has stopped and the processing can go no further. As Shirer and Jesus found out, to argue with such a person is futile because they do not have the capability to consider information outside the realm of what has been told to them; for if they were to consider such information, it would threaten to destroy a world view that has kept them safe and secure within the system in which they find themselves. In such instances, it is a means of self-preservation to stop the mind's processing at a point defined by that system.   .

People who rely on doctrine, propaganda and blind faith for their knowledge will never have the ability to answer logic with logic and will always rely on silence, personal attack, repetition of the doctrine and propaganda, censorship, banishment, cancellation and all the other means for combating logic in order to keep their false thinking in place without disturbance.

The last thing a master illusionist with power wants is an individual with unlimited information and knowledge because that would be the death knell for their cushy set-up as the wealthy and powerful subject matter experts of our world. All the corrupt, power abusing politicians, academics, scientists and CEOs who seem to be surrounding us now would soon find themselves out of jobs if the floodgates of information were open for everyone to access. Hitler knew this very well and it is why propaganda played such a prominent role in his regime. He knew he had to control the information flow in order to limit the German citizen's knowledge to what he wanted them to know; and what he wanted them to know was a purely fictitious version of reality arising out of his own corrupted world view and self-interests.

The chief priest, Caiaphas, also knew he had to control the information flow. He knew if people began to learn the truth of the scriptures that Jesus was teaching, they would realize they didn't need the Pharisees telling them what kind of choices to make because they were quite capable of making their own choices.

Knowing the truth of our existence and knowing how evil operates in the illusion of rationalizations, lies and blame gives us the ability to see the truth of all things. No longer will you accept the lies told to you by people with a false consciousness who occupy positions of power and who are willing to abuse that power by lying, deceiving and using other people as objects to achieve their selfish goals. This is what Jesus meant when he said he is the way, the truth and the light. He wasn't talking about himself. He was talking about the capacity we all have to create a life where we prosper in truth and do not allow ourselves to be fooled by minds that have been corrupted. That is the only way to freedom and prosperity.

I always go back to the Garden of Eden allegory because it gets to the core of the human mind and how it gets corrupted in this physical world in which we must survive. Let's use the example of Adam and Eve to illustrate how one gets caught up in what Jesus calls sin that cannot be forgiven. Eve knows instinctively that it is wrong to eat the fruit, but she wants it so badly. The only way she is able to override her inborn spirit of truth is by telling herself that eating the fruit is actually a good thing for her to do. She does this by changing her thinking. Before the snake comes along, Eve knows two things to be true: 1) She can eat the fruit of any tree except the two trees in the middle of the garden, and 2) If she eats from either of the two trees in the middle of the garden, she will die. After talking to the snake and changing her thinking, her new thoughts about the fruit become: 1) Why did God put a tree with such pleasing fruit there if he didn't want it to be eaten, and 2) The tree's fruit is desirable for gaining wisdom. God just didn't want her to have that wisdom.

What Eve did was to take the input in the form of the Garden's law and use her consciousness to change that input so that it would create output more in her favor. The snake convinces her it is a physical death that God is referring to and tells her she most certainly will not die by eating the fruit. However, a physical death is not the kind of death God means when God tells her not to eat fruit from the tree of knowledge of good and evil. It is the death of her consciousness of true and false (good and evil). It is the erasure of the law of her inner being that Jesus talked about with the Pharisees who blasphemed against the holy Spirit and it is the lack of a sense of guilt of the Nazi soldiers over brutalizing and killing so many of their fellow men and women because they were just following orders. In all instances, they created a space in their minds that was never meant to exist in the first place and every choice made after that 'creation' produced destructive, soul-killing garbage for its output.

The process Eve uses to change her thinking is called rationalization and it is what everyone does to justify actions their gut is telling them are wrong. Most of the time this is not even a conscious process. It is something we do subconsciously and are not even aware we have done it. The only way to correct this wrong thinking is by examining ourselves in an honest way to determine the real reasons why we are thinking what we are thinking, saying what we are saying and doing what we are doing. Unfortunately, we have come to rely too heavily on our criminal and civil statutes to guide us in right behavior. The problem with this approach is that there is always a way for people who so desire to skirt around the law or, if powerful enough, to disregard the law entirely or write a new one better suited to their goals.

Eve makes the Garden a very dicey environment when she finds she has the power to change the rule of not eating the fruit to one more amenable to her own desires. Instead of letting what she knows to be true guide her, ie. the fruit from the tree of knowledge of good and evil is not to be eaten; she convinces herself God is lying. She turns the tables on truth and her belief becomes whatever she wants it to be. In this case, it is that God does not want her to eat the fruit because then she would become just like him and he wanted to keep that knowledge all to himself.

The Garden gets turned upside-down by Eve's rejection of reality and truth in favor of the illusion (delusion) of her own mind. Adam can conform or not but if he does not, he knows he will suffer some very real and painful punishments. Eve is what appears real to him at the moment she stands before him with fruit in hand telling him to take a bite. He knows it doesn't look right that she is wearing a fig leaf when she has never worn one before and the whole thing doesn't feel quite right to him but he goes ahead anyway and does what she tells him to do knowing it is probably wrong and also knowing that he would rather live well with Eve calling the shots than stake his future on a conscience that can be so easily manipulated and silenced. It was a decision he would live to regret.

I think that the Garden/Creation allegory makes clear that is is our responsibility to make sure the information we process is true, so that the output (our behavior) is based upon a realistic view of ourselves and our surroundings. Using the words of Jesus, Eve 'blasphemes against the holy Spirit' by using false reasoning to talk herself into doing something she instinctively knows is wrong. She thereby commits unforgiven sin because her thinking has changed in such a way that if faced with a similar situation again, she would act in the same corrupt way because she successfully convinced herself that her corrupted thinking process (represented by the snake's argument) was right.

Sin That Cannot Be Forgiven According to Jesus

Jesus first introduces us to the concept of sin that cannot be forgiven in Matthew, chapter 12, where he has just cured a person who is blind and mute and the crowd is astonished, wondering if he indeed may be the Messiah. The Pharisees, like all power abusers, are jealous of Jesus' popularity and instead of giving him the credit he deserves, they try to demean him in front of the crowd by saying it's through Satan that Jesus was able to cure the man. This is an intentional lie and Jesus calls them out on it by saying, "*If I drive out demons by Beelzebul, by whom do your own people drive them out?*"

Jesus uses the Pharisees' attempt to assassinate his character as an opportunity to tell the crowd about the true nature of sin, of which the Pharisees are guilty, but of which they are totally unaware they are guilty. The passage in full reads as follows:

> "Then they brought to him a demoniac who was blind and mute. He cured the mute person so that he could speak and see. All the crowd was astounded, and said, "Could this perhaps be the Son of David?" But when the Pharisees heard this, they said, "This man drives out demons only by the power of Beelzebul, the prince of demons." But he knew what they were thinking and said to them, "Every kingdom divided against itself will be laid waste, and no town or house divided against itself will stand. And if Satan drives out Satan, he is divided against himself; how, then, will his kingdom stand? And if I drive out demons by Beelzebul, by whom do your own people drive them out? Therefore they will be your judges. But if it is by the Spirit of God that I drive out demons, then the kingdom of God has come upon you.[159]

This passage doesn't say that Jesus heard what they said, it says that Jesus knew what they were thinking. What this tells us is that Jesus isn't scolding them for their behavior. He is correcting them at the level of their thoughts. The energetic level of thought is the level that all of Jesus' teachings should be applied because they absolutely do not work at the physical level of behavior, and quite possibly are destructive in most instances when they are applied at the physical level of behavior.

Jesus' teachings regarding 'turn the other cheek,' 'love your enemies,' 'a kingdom divided against itself cannot stand,' 'reaping what you sow,' 'judgment,' and the 'the golden rule' are all logical conclusions based upon the laws of energy that I discuss in a later chapter. Jesus never intended his teachings to dictate behavior like our laws do. They were meant to work on the energy of our mind's emotions and thoughts. It is why all his teachings seem counter intuitive in an ego conscious world where the focus is on the physical body and brain rather than on the energy without which the physical brain and body would not exist. Ego has turned our thinking inside-out and upside-down. In order to correct one's thinking, a person has to switch their perspective and then figure out how to make Jesus' message applicable to energy rather than physical behavior. It is almost like learning a new language.

For instance, when Jesus tells us to turn the other cheek, he is not giving us a strategy for handling people who are mean. He is telling us that nothing in the external world should ever affect our inner being. We should always remain single minded in following the commandments of our consciousness by staying focused on truth and the reality that a person is not their outward physical existence. People are consciousness and as such, their thoughts and emotions make them the individuals they are.

It all makes so much sense when we shift our focus to consciousness as the essential part of our being rather than placing it on borders, culture, titles, education, social class, race, nationality, sexuality, sexual orientation and all the other ego created separations that place us into groups by which we are defined. Group separations will always nurture an environment where one group can demonize another for purposes of gaining an edge. If everyone was viewed as an individual of consciousness instead of a German, American, black, white, Chinese, terrorist, patriot, woman, man and so on, it would create an environment where peace could actually become a reality.

Jesus was not speaking to groups of people when he commanded them to love their enemies and turn their cheeks. He was speaking to you, individually, he was speaking to me and he was speaking to the abuser. He was addressing the states of our individual minds. He was telling targets to never let someone else define them. Turn your other cheek by keeping your confidence intact and your love for yourself strong.

The real problem with the Pharisees was with the way they were thinking and it was reflected in the way they behaved. Their consciousness of true and false had gone haywire because of all the lies they told themselves in order to make themselves feel morally superior to everyone else. They were applying one set of rules to themselves and another to Jesus, which is why Jesus asks them how their own people are able to drive out demons through God, but when Jesus does it, it is by Satan.

In the case of sin that cannot be forgiven, Jesus tells the Pharisees in Matthew 12:31-32, "Every sin and blasphemy will be forgiven. And whoever speaks a word against the Son of Man will be forgiven; but whoever speaks against the holy Spirit will not be forgiven, either in this age or in the age to come." A person guilty of sin that cannot be forgiven doesn't feel the need to correct the wrong assumptions, rationalizations and justifications of their false consciousness. Under such circumstances, they never feel the need to ask the person they've wronged for forgiveness because they are unaware they have done anything wrong. Jesus tells us in John 10:33 that man can forgive sin. This is what he meant. When we make a change in our thinking that aligns us more to truth, then we have been forgiven. We have repented when we have given up the frame of mind that caused us to have wrong motives (sin) and we are saved through correcting our thinking in a way that makes us want to do the right thing the next time around, no matter the consequences. This is not an occasional process like making a New Year's resolution. It is a daily, moment-by-moment process that takes place with every thought we have, every word we say and every action we take.

The sin of the Pharisees wasn't in the lies they told out loud. It was in the irrational thought process that prompted them to lie about Jesus in the first place. Jesus knew they wanted to undermine him to make the crowd think less of him and his abilities. They intentionally wanted to harm him and the lie was their way to do it. Put in terms of cause and effect, the lie was the effect of their cause to diminish Jesus in the eyes of the people who hung on his every word. Satan cannot drive out Satan, but Satan can certainly feed Satan in the case of a false consciousness seeking revenge, power or control over another person's consciousness. And the Pharisees are nothing if not the perfect example of how a false consciousness feeds the demon, rather than chasing it out.

Making the Two into One

The first sentence of the Gnostic Gospel of Thomas says, "These are the secret words which the living Jesus taught and which Judas Thomas Didymos wrote down." There are a total of 110 sayings and saying 22 reads as follows: "When you make the two one and make the inside like the outside and the outside like the inside and the above like the below, and that you might make the male and the female be one and the same, so that the male might not be male nor the female be female, when you make eyes in place of an eye and a hand in place of a hand and a foot in place of a foot, an image in place of an image - then you will enter [the kingdom]."

Eve refuses to make the two into one when she refuses to get back to her original programming. She chooses to lie to herself in the face of truth and that choice prevents her from ever eating from the Tree of Life.[160] Sin is a choice and choice belongs to the individual. It is up to all of us individually and always has been. That is why knowledge and free speech is so important. It is the only way to truly make informed choices for ourselves. As I wrote earlier, he who controls the information flow controls all because information creates knowledge and unlimited knowledge creates unlimited possibilities. If we are to apply the scientific method to our own minds so that we can stay grounded in truth and reality, then no information should be off the table.

The Spiritual Message of Love is not Enough

As Jesus taught it, our natural state of being is one of joy, peace and abundance. The upside-down opposite of our natural state of being is unhappiness, anxiety and scarcity. Power abusers must keep the people they control in the upside-down mode of survival because survival is the only environment in which they can thrive. Hitler turned the natural state upside-down when he put the population he ruled in survival mode without them even realizing it. They were made to feel thankful they had jobs – boring, repetitive and meaningless jobs created by the bureaucracy. They were slaves without knowing they were slaves just as much as the Israelites who Moses led out of Egypt were slaves who didn't know they were slaves. That is why they could grumble to Moses about how hard it was and look longingly at their days in Egypt where at least they had food on the table.

In the story, Moses gave them complete and utter freedom in which they could create whatever future they could envision and all they could envision was the slavery they were accustomed to in Egypt. That is because their rulers back in Egypt took their life force from them and made them content to be mindless and grumbling automatons who, when they actually tasted freedom, were unable to embrace it and create a land of milk and honey for themselves and their families. If another generation had not come along during those forty years in the wilderness who had never been enslaved and who were brought up with knowledge of the rules of consciousness, the slave masters in Egypt would have gotten their slaves back voluntarily and the Israelites would never have entered the promised land.

Jesus gave his followers who were enslaved under the Roman Empire and their Pharisaic leadership the same message Moses gave the Israelites and the crowds of people who were coming to hear Jesus speak were beginning to embrace it. If not for being stopped in his tracks by Caiaphas and the Council, Jesus' message would have spread exponentially.

The spiritual message of love is not enough. In fact, the power abusers themselves love that message because it is so ill-defined and new agey. What exactly does it mean to love one another? What exactly does that entail if that is all the information one is given? Yes, Jesus told his disciples to love one another when he was saying goodbye to them at the last supper. Outside of that moment, Jesus actually spoke very little about love.

Love is a natural outpouring of a consciousness that knows the truth. However; that is different from making love the goal. The goal should always be to live in reality and truth, out of which will come the positive manifestations of peace, love, justice, equality, fearlessness, courage, fortitude, motivation, dedication, discipline, logic, compassion, empathy, etc. Jesus was loving but he was not all about love. He was all about respecting a person's right to choose how they conduct their lives within the parameters of the laws of consciousness. Hypocrisy was abhorrent to him. The idea that the Pharisees could impose restrictive rules and regulations on people that they themselves had the audacity not to follow got his blood boiling. You can feel his pent-up rage when he goes after them with a vengeance in Matthew 23:3-36, calling them all kinds of names that accurately reflect their blindness to their own evil and their willingness to lead every other Jew into the same pit of hell to which they were headed. I cannot help but think that Jesus knew exactly the danger he was putting himself in by speaking so bluntly to the hypocritical 'evildoers' but he was incapable of acting any differently. This is where his love comes in. His love was the real kind of love that courageously speaks truth knowing that truth is the only way to improvement. His was not the fake kind of love that compliments with shallow expressions meant to build self esteem. He practiced tough love that demolishes ignorance and weakness so that a person's true character in consciousness can come through and grow stronger on a foundation of knowledge and truth.

Too many people practice a false kind of love that requires no effort. They will withhold the truth for fear of hurting a person's feelings and avoiding conflict. I notice this particularly with regard to groups that define themselves as spiritual. Many of their members will purposely carry an aura of peace, serenity and calmness about them. You can see it in their soft-spoken manner and gentle movements. I felt myself trying it to put it on the few times when I attended a spiritual center and listened to them talk about the power of positive vibrations and love to change the world. I would agree with them that there are vibrations created by nurturing a positive and calm nature, but they are created within the individual mind to produce greater clarity. When I attain those moments of clarity, I usually want to write because nurturing the positive qualities of my nature usually brings along with it a new idea or desire to create. I am able to give my son better advice. I do not get depressed as often and when I do begin to feel down, I have the tools for snapping out of it. In my interactions with other people, I am conscious of how I treat them. Am I not interrupting? Am I listening to what they are saying or letting my mind drift off elsewhere? Am I not getting angry when I have to wait longer in line or when someone honks at me for not making the right turn on red? All these actions arise out of a desire to treat other people with respect, not love. It is honoring them as human beings and realizing they have faults and problems just like me. Do I love them? Some yes and some no. It is impossible to love everyone because some people are unlovable. How could Jesus love the Pharisees who constantly stalked, harassed and eventually killed him? How could Martin Luther King love the people who made him sit in the back of the bus? We can love the fact that they have a common consciousness with us of which they are unaware, but we cannot and should not try to love how they are choosing to manifest that consciousness in a false and negative manner.

Jesus was called to teach the truth about our consciousness of the good and the evil / the false and the true / the illusion and the reality. That is the symbolism of the Holy Spirit descending upon him like a dove after his baptism. [Luke 3:22] He was fully conscious of the nature of good and evil and his forty days in the wilderness was his own personal testing ground to ensure he could resist the pressures he knew he would encounter so that he could always practice what he was preaching. The word 'compromise' was not in his vocabulary. He stayed true to his consciousness of truth by calling out the Pharisees every chance he could.

Hoping our vibrations of love will change the world is unreal and delusional. The time has come to get real. The treatment of people around the world is deteriorating. There are constant wars with no end in sight. Democracy is creating totalitarian regimes that subjugate women because the populace who voted the leadership into power believes women should be subjugated. Business leaders in our own country are praising the business practices of China even as the country keeps much of its labor force working in slave-like conditions. Conditions haven't changed much since Jesus' day because we all keep hoping things will get better. The reality is that conditions won't improve until human beings individually improve. It has taken so much hard work to bring myself to a state of inner strength and transformation after realizing my own false consciousness was personally causing me so much anxiety, depression and negative stress and was manifesting in behavior that was harmful to both myself and the people around me. It is daily, emotionally strenuous work. I didn't choose to undergo this inner work because a group of loving people sent loving vibrations my way. I had to read and learn and talk to others to get at the solutions that worked for me. It was time consuming and mentally exhausting. It required me to take an honest look at myself, faults and all, and begin the long process of trying to change them. I'm still trying.

Now multiply the experience of one individual (me) who hasn't even begun to reach her full potential by the several billion or so people on this planet who need to go through a similar process to come to the truth that enlightened people like the Buddha, Martin Luther King, Jesus and others have come to. It is daunting and the only way to approach a daunting job is to break it down into its individual tasks and approach them one-by-one. There is no way around it. If the world is to make a positive change, all individuals must do the hard work of becoming wise people of character and integrity individually. They need to see the benefit of being this way rather than caving into the overall corruption and ignorance of the group in power, whether it be in their governments, schools, workplaces, neighborhoods or families.

To me, the only way to get people to see the benefit of doing the painstaking work of improving themselves is to reveal the overall picture to them and make them aware of the long-term consequences of their actions. Jesus tried doing this and was stopped dead in his tracks by the Pharisees who were fearful of losing their power. Then afterward, his legacy in the form of his teachings was lost to a large degree by a Christian church run by powerful men who had their own agendas. They chose the information that would go in the New Testament Gospels of Jesus and the information that would stay out. It allowed them to shape the message around the religion rather than letting the message determine the religion. It is time for the religion to come out of the hands of the church and into the street. Jesus taught in the fields, mountains and towns where there were people who needed the tools he gave them to become healthy and balanced individuals. Jesus was not about religion. He was about helping men and women find their purpose and fulfill their destinies and he did that by being honest with them and telling them about the truth of their human nature.

Truth Is Our Way Out of the Matrix

Logic dictates that all beings who are equal be treated equally. To accept less is to accept less of the potential contained within each of us. Our purpose as human beings is to perfect the trinity of our being so that we can change the course of our world and begin moving forward on an evolutionary track that fulfills the destiny of all men and women, not just the ones who are positioned well within existing structures that benefit them to the exclusion of people the existing structures do not benefit.

The Pharisees could not allow people in the Jewish community to see their potential because it would have become glaringly clear to them how little they needed the Pharisees or their laws to tell them how to think, what to say and how to act. The reason we are like them and the Israelites before them in thinking we need other people telling us what we should do is because our minds have been trained since birth to believe the illusion; and the hens running the hen house in the form of authority figures we are told to obey without question are the ones training us to believe it. The only way that will ever change is when each individual on their own takes up the responsibility of training themselves in the truth - the truth of the Bible, the truth of Jesus and the truth of how this world works.

As more and more people hear the truth and act on it courageously, things will change for the better. The only people afraid of the truth are those people with a vested interest in telling lies and keeping us fearful. I keep hearing Christian ministers preach on the dangers of bringing religions together. That is because the power structure of the Christian church has a vested interest in keeping doctrine the way it is. The power structure of the Muslim community has a vested interest in keeping doctrine the way it is. When reality and truth get in the way of their false doctrines, they turn to the old stand by: "Have faith, my children." What? Faith in unreality? Faith in things that are impossible – like the bringing back of a physical body from death? Faith in not viewing women as equal to men? I no longer fall for any of it. I see the power structure behind the curtain.

They like to talk about the end of times. Well, if there is an end of times it will be the end of the good times they have enjoyed fooling us and appeasing our desire to hear a positive message that doesn't embrace the whole truth. The Old Testament never mentions Satan. The God of the Old Testament is the consciousness of good (true) and evil (false) that its characters 'choose' to follow in determining how they think and therefore act. If nothing else, the Bible is an instruction book on how we can choose to think and therefore act in a positive way that benefits ourselves and others - or in a negative way that benefits our own self-interests at the expense of anyone who gets in the way of those interests.

In our evolutionary war between what has been labeled as good and evil, evil is winning and will always win until we throw off the cover of our false consciousness and reveal the cruel reality of an enemy that insidiously poses itself to the world as something good and admirable. Knowledge, logic, rationality and truth are the weapons of warfare in this war and the battle cry is Jesus' persistent reminder to his followers and disciples telling them, "Anyone who has ears, ought to hear." (Matthew 11:15, Matthew 13:43, Mark 4:9, Luke 8:8)

Content of Our Character

Hitler surrounded himself with men who had no morals because he knew those were the kind of men he needed around him to achieve his goals. It is too bad the New Testament gospels got all garbled with the do and don't letters of Paul – letters that continue to be the focus of many modern-day churches. I have attached as Appendix II all the rules that Paul imposed on his church members. He set himself up as the parent instructing his children on what they should and should not do. The rules are totally from his own head without any relation whatsoever to Jesus.

As the list of rules contained in Appendix II illustrates, Paul was all about command and control. In contrast, Jesus was all about the content of our character rather than the imposition of rules that can be so easily manipulated and used to serve the interests of some very bad people with no character. The gospels of Jesus make clear that Jesus was first and foremost a teacher and his temple was his mind. He sought to keep it pure by staying as rational and logical as possible by remaining grounded in the universal laws of consciousness. He wasn't interested in church building. He was all about helping men and women find their purpose and fulfill their destinies and he did that by being honest with them and telling them about the truth of their human nature as the mind of God.

Although Jesus taught with the confines of the temple, he also got out into the neighboring towns where Gentiles, Samaritans and other non-Jews were flocking to hear him. That's because his message was not religious in the true sense of the word. He was translating universal truths from the Bible that had been hijacked by the Pharisees and made into a money-making operation within the physical structure of the temple. The early Christian church had the opportunity to right this wrong, but it was also run by power brokers with their own agendas. They chose what would be included in the New Testament and rejected any writings that conflicted with the message they wanted to give. They chose to include the letters of Paul that falsely said that Jesus is the only son of God who offers redemption to those who accept him as savior. The message that Jesus himself gave on salvation through self-examination, which is the focus of more recently discovered gospels like the Gospel of Mary, James and Thomas, is all but lost in the New Testament as it exists today. It is only when all those gospels are taken together with the four gospels of Jesus (Matthew, Mark, Luke and John) that we get a full picture of Jesus' own belief system.

Chapter 9
The Myth Created
by the Impostor Apostle

Hitler was so successful at taking over Germany because he created an alternate reality that I call illusion. All the tactics he used didn't just distort truth — they denied it completely in his conscious effort to create an environment more conducive to what he wanted to accomplish. It was his goal to create a new order in the world where a master race of Germans would control the globe, writing the following in *Mein Kampf*:

> "We all feel that in the distant future many may be faced with problems which can be solved only by a superior race of human beings, a race destined to become master of all the other peoples and which will have at its disposal the means and resources of the whole world."[161]

and

> "If we would transform our ideal picture of the People"s State into a reality we shall have to keep independent of the forces that now control public life and seek for new forces that will be ready and capable of taking up the fight for such an ideal. For a fight it will have to be, since the first objective will not be to build up the idea of the People"s State but rather to wipe out the Jewish State which is now in

existence. <u>As so often happens in the course of history, the main difficulty is not to establish a new order of things but to clear the ground for its establishment.</u> Prejudices and egotistic interests join together in forming a common front against the new idea and in trying by every means to prevent its triumph, because it is disagreeable to them or threatens their existence. That is why the protagonist of the new idea is unfortunately, in spite of his desire for constructive work, compelled to wage a destructive battle first, in order to abolish the existing state of affairs."[162]

Hitler was caretaker of Germany in his leadership role. He had no right to re-make Germany in his image just as Eve has no right to re-make the Garden in her image. It was in his own revengeful self-interest to wipe out what he perceived as the Jewish State to build the Peoples State his false consciousness envisioned. The new version of the world he wanted to create suited his agenda, but it was at the expense of so many millions of people for whom there was no place in the new physical order.

The process Hitler wanted to use to make way for his world vision was not an easy one given that the ground Hitler was operating upon was a world of self-determining, sovereign, nation-states. The autocratic state Hitler wanted to create was in opposition to the democratic country of Germany where all its citizens were afforded equal rights under the Weimar Constitution. Obviously those rules, Constitution and rights were what needed to be destroyed to make way for Hitler's new order. Clearing the ground was most definitely difficult and would involve aggressive war and the elimination of any person or group who got in the way.

Some people view Hitler as the anti-Christ and he is, but only in the sense that he gave us the playbook for creating illusion on a mass scale. However, Hitler did not create that playbook. He got it from the

Communists (Social Democrats) that he studied so compulsively after being made a target of destruction himself by a group of them at his workplace in Vienna. But it was not the Communists who created the playbook either. It has been around since King Saul used it against the future King David and probably as long as the human species has evolved from its time in the animal kingdom into conscious and communicative human beings.

After reading *Mein Kampf* and the Nuremberg trial transcripts, I can no longer turn a blind eye to the truth that what we label as good and evil is a matter of perspective. In Nazi Germany, the Nazis were good and Jews were evil because they were perceived as the cause of all of Germany's problems. Hitler always framed the persecution of the Jews in terms of handling the Jewish problem. All power abusers and bullies portray their targets of abuse as the problem in the relationship and then use their more powerful position in the relationship to convince everyone else that the target is the problem as well. The perception of a non-conscious population that does the cost-benefit analysis based upon their external environment, rather than any internal set of values and rules that they will not compromise, is easily manipulated by the people in power who control the information flow and can pass laws and exert societal pressures that make it detrimental not to conform to the party line. This was certainly the dynamic in Hitler's Germany.

Jesus was not immune from the dynamic. In the workplace of the Jewish temple, Jesus was doing the work of Satan and the Pharisees were doing the work of God. The incident from Jesus' own life which I discuss in chapter eight on sin that cannot be forgiven is a perfect example of how people use projection, either consciously or subconsciously, to degrade people they consider a threat to their power. Jesus had just cured a person and the crowd who witnessed the healing started believing that Jesus was the Messiah. Since the Pharisees couldn't tolerate that, they accuse Jesus of using satanic means to cure the man.

The process of projecting our own inadequacies and faults onto people we want to minimize and demean was one that Hitler was so fond of using to destroy his perceived enemies. In fact, in a speech Hitler gave in April 1932, he lies about this very incident to demonize the Jews he is out to destroy saying, " "We know that the Jew, whether he is baptized as a Protestant or as a Catholic, remains a Jew. Why can you not realize this, you Protestant clergymen, you Catholic priests, you who have scales before your eyes and serve the God of the Jews, who is not the God of Love but the God of Hate. Why do you not listen to Christ, who said to the Jews: 'You are the children of the Devil'."[163]

This is a complete and utter lie. Jesus never said that. Jesus was himself a Jew. However, once statements like that are out there, they gain a life of their own, particularly in an authoritarian environment. Instead of lying about what Jesus said, Hitler should have taken it to heart and applied it to his own life and mind. When Jesus responded to the Pharisees' character assassination of him by telling them that Satan cannot drive out Satan, he was basically saying you do not fight a fire with more fire. You have to apply an agent that puts out the fire.

In *Mein Kampf*, Hitler describes having feelings of depression, anguish and hate in the aftermath of his firing. However, like his work colleagues, Hitler was very egoistic and obstinate and liked the thrill of the fight; but unlike them, he lacked any power. I think Hitler wanted to obtain that kind of power and saw that their tactics could give it to him. When Hitler adopted the tactics of the Social Democrats that were used so effectively against him by his colleagues in the building trade, he was driving out Satan with Satan. A more sane and rational approach would have been to denounce those tactics, knowing how much harm they caused to his own psyche.

I don't believe that experience in Hitler's workplace ever left him. He became revengeful and he never worked on getting past that revenge. He fed into it with his hatred for all things social democratic. His hatred of the Jews arose out of his irrationality. Since Jews owned the newspaper spouting Social Democratic ideas, he imprinted his hatred of the Communists on all Jews as well.[164] It was not an ideological fight he waged with Communists. Hitler was himself a socialist. No. The fight was a very personal one and he became obsessed with learning all he could about Social Democracy in an attempt to understand the men who destroyed his wellbeing so that he could turn the tables on them and destroy them in a similar manner.

It was very easy for Hitler to nurture those feelings of revenge and hatred by matching them in kind against the people he felt were responsible for his misery. In fact, an-eye-for-an-eye revenge feels quite natural for anyone who has suffered an emotional and/or psychological assault at the hands of another human being. After all, according to science, for every action there is an equal and opposite reaction. What we forget, and what Jesus taught, is that in cases of negative emotions and thoughts, the opposite reaction should be something that destroys (puts out) those negative emotions and thoughts. From personal experience I can tell you that the last thing a person wants to do is endure the hard work of nurturing positive thoughts and emotions when their mind is caught in a constant drumbeat of negative thoughts about the perpetrators and a minute-by-minute, repetitive replay of the events that are causing them so much mental anguish. It takes extremely hard work over an extended period of time to recognize the wisdom of the strategy for combating the war that is going on in our minds at such times; much less to follow it when all we can think about is how much we hate the perpetrators, how undeserved their actions towards us were and how much we want them to suffer in kind.

Jesus' teachings are very hard. They go counter to our feelings in many instances. We desire revenge for people who have hurt us, yet Jesus tells us about the importance of retaining the integrity of our soul by not feeding emotional violence with further violence. Seeking revenge is like Satan driving out Satan. The cycle of abuse stops when a victim decides he/she will not continue the behavior done to them with someone else.

I think Hitler's obstinacy may have served him very well if only he had chosen not to drive out Satan with Satan. He was very passionate when he believed in something. He was also very goal-driven, well-spoken and talented. I truly believe he could have achieved so much in his lifetime and created a positive legacy if at that critical time in his life, he had mustered the strength to use all his book knowledge to heal himself and his mind rather than taking the destructive path he did.

I have called Hitler a master of illusion throughout this book. However, another way to put it is that he was a master of perception. If victory in the war had been his, he would have continued to use his propaganda machine, oratory skills and power over the press and history books to create the perception that he was the savior of humanity his over-sized ego envisioned, rather than the most evil man in history he has become. Unless we individually acquire the ability to cut through the lies and manipulations that have changed our mind's programming from its natural state, in order to perceive another more realistic side to the stories we are told and tell ourselves; then we will never be able to discern the truth for ourselves about our world and people who have been painted as either sinners or saints, villains or heroes.

I am well aware that when most people hear the name, Jesus, they want to run for the hills. But that is because the Jesus they have heard about is a product of perception manipulation. With mobbings, legacies are destroyed, destinies are ruined and good reputations are forever tarnished. Some of the words the Pharisees used to describe Jesus while he was alive were glutton, drunkard, crazy and impostor. Unless someone comes along later to restore a person's legacy and reputation, it remains as the perpetrators defined it during the mobbing.

Some would argue that the man who has become known as the Apostle Paul, along with Jesus's disciples, restored Jesus's legacy. However, I would argue that they forever changed it to the great detriment of themselves and humanity at large. In their teachings, they placed the holy Spirit - what Jesus called the spirit of Truth in John 16:13 - in an entity outside of the mind that miraculously enters a person's body with the declaration that a person accepts Jesus as their savior. I write in *The Mobbing of Jesus Christ* that I believe the reason for this was self-preservation. They saw Stephen, a follower of the Way [of Jesus] who was teaching the true consciousness message of Jesus, stoned to death as the Pharisee named Saul, later known as Paul, looked on. [See Acts 7:1-60]

Paul is the man who built up the early Christian Church as it remains today after claiming he experienced a vision from Jesus. As the story goes, a Pharisee named Paul heard the voice of Jesus during his travel to Damascus while he was still known as Saul. He changed his name to Paul after his alleged conversion. [Acts 13:9] According to Acts 9:1-5, Saul was on his way to Damascus "breathing murderous threats against the disciples of the Lord," with the intent of bringing any followers of Jesus he found back to Jerusalem in chains. At some point during his journey a light suddenly flashed around him and he heard a voice say to him, "Saul, Saul, why are you persecuting me?" When Saul asked who was asking, the voice told him it was Jesus. Saul claims that the men who were traveling with him also heard the voice. [See Acts 9:7]

That was the extent of the alleged vision we are given and yet the Church has given this story the credibility it needs to make Saul, better known as Paul, a saint whose written letters to the churches he founded make up a majority of the New Testament gospels and serve as the foundation for its doctrine. This is true even given the fact that Paul's story about the vision changes when he later appears in Court. In court, the story became that he alone heard the voice.[See Acts 22:9] I presume this story change came about because the court may have requested to hear from the witnesses. And I also assume his story change indicates that he was unable to produce the non-existent witnesses.

Either the story Paul told the disciples and his gentile followers of his Jesus vision was true or the story he told the Court was true. Paul cannot have it both ways. Either way, one of those stories was a lie. It is my belief he lied to the disciples and his gentile followers when he said there were others with him who heard the voice because he wanted to give his vision account more credibility. Apparently it worked because when he first met with Jesus' disciples in Jerusalem and tried to join them as a disciple, "they were all afraid of him not believing he was a disciple." It wasn't until he went back to the disciples with a man named Barnabus and told them his story about hearing Jesus that they accepted him into the flock. [See Acts 9:26-28]

Apparently, that story was good enough for the disciples of Jesus; it was good enough for the gentile followers who filled Paul's churches and it has been good enough for all the Christian churches ever since who have used it as validation for Paul and his false message.

As a realist myself and a seeker of truth, I find that acceptance to be absolutely mind-blowing, especially given the fact that in all his letters, Paul never expresses regret or shame at his killing of innocent men and women or says he is sorry for it. An inconsistent story about hearing the voice of Jesus has given an unrepentant killer the legacy of a saint and his teachings the foundation for a world-wide religion that has people essentially believing a myth. That is bad enough, but it is a myth that has had eternal consequences for billions of souls since its introduction.

If the church was not blinded by the indoctrination of Paul's saintliness over the hundreds of years since his claimed 'sudden conversion' it might allow for the possibility that Saul was the perfect candidate for the campaign of misdirection the Pharisees wanted to conduct to turn people away from the powerful consciousness teachings of Jesus.

It is my belief that there was a huge misdirection campaign instigated against Jesus after the crucifixion and Paul was chosen as the one to direct the campaign. According to the texts forbidden by the church as heresy, there were several witnesses other than the apostles who saw Jesus alive after the crucifixion. In the following passage from *The Gospel of Nicodemus, formerly called the Acts of Pontius Pilate.* it says three of those witnesses were paid off by the chief priests and then escorted out of Jerusalem never to return:

> 18 But a certain priest Phinees, Ada a schoolmaster, and a Levite, named Ageus, they three came from Galilee to Jerusalem, and told the chief priests and all who were in the synagogues, saying, 19 We have seen Jesus, whom ye crucified, talking with his eleven disciples, and sitting in the midst of them in Mount Olivet, and saying to them, 20 Go forth into the whole world, preach the Gospel to all nations,

baptizing them in the name of the Father, and the Son, and the Holy Ghost; and whosoever shall believe and bebaptized, shall be saved. 25 Then the chief priests immediately rose up, and holding the book of the law in their hands, conjured these men, saying, Ye shall no more hereafter declare those things which ye have spoken concerning Jesus. 26 <u>And they gave them a large sum of money, and sent other persons along with them, who should conduct them to their own country, that they might not by any means make any stay at Jerusalem.</u>[165]

Also, as indicated in the passage below, the chief priests, Annas and Caiaphas, met with the Jews who were told by the soldiers at the tomb that the stone sealing the tomb had been rolled away by an angel:

27 Then the Jews did assemble all together, and having expressed the most lamentable concern said, What is this extraordinary thing which is come to pass in Jerusalem? 28 But Annas and Caiaphas comforted them, saying, Why should we believe the soldiers who guarded the sepulchre of Jesus, in telling us, that an angel rolled away the stone from the door of the sepulchre? 29 Perhaps his own disciples told them this, and gave them money that they should say so, and they themselves took away the body ofJesus. 30 Besides, consider this, that there is no credit to begiven to foreigners, because they also took a large sum of us, and they have declared to us according to the instructions which we gave them. <u>They must either be faithful to us or to the disciples of Jesus</u>.

Even though the first passage above indicates that the witnesses were paid off for their silence, the fact remained that they could still say something. Caiaphas and Annas realize that fact when they say in the second passage, "They must either be faithful to us or to the disciples of Jesus." Caiaphas and Annas were well aware that their plot to kill Jesus failed and that he was still around to cause them trouble. This was a huge loose end, to say the least. They knew that people talk and that the witnesses could always choose to spread the word that the disciples told them; ie. that 'an angel' moved the rock from Jesus' sepulchre. They had to cover all their bases. In their cunning, I believe they decided to use the angel story to their advantage. They knew no angel moved that rock and they also knew that the dead do not come back to life. It was obvious to them that Jesus somehow survived the cross and was up and around walking and talking to his disciples. They failed in their mission to kill him. So, what do you do when faced with an enemy who will not go away? You defang them by changing their message; thereby dissolving any threat that message may have on your control and power.

It is not long after that Saul/Paul, a Pharisee, Roman citizen and killer of Jesus's followers shows up to claim he is a new man after hearing a voice claiming to be that of Jesus utter one sentence to him, "Why are you persecuting me?" After this encounter, he leads us to believe he is a new man in Christ through his letters that comprise the majority of the Bible's New Testament. In those letters, he changed the entire message from self-awareness as the antidote to unforgiven sin to a false salvation message where one man (Jesus) is sacrificed for the sins of one man (Adam). Saul/Paul tells us that if we merely accept Jesus as our savior, then through his sacrifice we will be forgiven of all our sins. He gives a message totally foreign to Jesus's consciousness teachings, using instead the 'resurrection' of Jesus as the means of salvation. The reasoning he uses to make his case for this method of salvation is based on his argument that Man (Adam) is an actual human being - the original human being that God created in the Garden and that he sinned. Through that one sin, all of humanity was condemned through the ages. Thus, God sent Jesus to die for that sin and thereby save mankind. One man for one man.

Does that argument sound familiar by now? I can continue explaining the absurdity of it, as I explained the absurdity of it when Hitler used it to justify killing millions of Jews and Caiaphas used it to justify killing Jesus. However, let me give you Saul/Paul's own words and let you decide for yourself the absurdity of turning an allegory into a fact and then basing an entire religion upon it.

In Romans 5:15, Saul/Paul writes:

"For if by that one person's transgression the many died, how much more did the grace of God and the gracious gift of the one person Jesus Christ, overflow for the many."

And in Romans 5:12-14, he writes:

"Therefore, just as through one person sin entered the world, and through sin, death and thus death came to all, inasmuch as all sinned - for up to the time of the law, sin was in the world, though sin is not accounted when there is no law. But death reigned from Adam to Moses, even over those who did not sin after the pattern of the trespass of Adam, who is the type of the one who was to come."

According to Paul, it was one man's death for one man's sin as a means of salvation for all. Thus, according to Paul, if we merely accept that Jesus is our savior through his sacrifice, then we will be forgiven of all our sins, now and forevermore.

What is most interesting is that the one man's death for one man's sin, which is the centerpiece of Paul's doctrine, is a blatant mischaracterization of what really happened. Paul says it was the Man, Adam, who first brought sin into the world when in actuality it was the Woman, Eve, who took the first bite from the fruit. However, I suppose one man's death for one woman's sin wouldn't fit in the male chauvinist world view. It had to be changed, which was not a problem because Saul/Paul was dealing with a group of people who didn't know any better. They depended on him to teach them. He could say whatever he wanted knowing very few, if any, would fact check what he said. After all, he was the authority in the law and the scriptures. And surprisingly enough, his indoctrination has held up through the ages with few people, if any, fact checking what he said.

However, there is one person who did fact check him and that was Jesus himself, in the flesh. There is evidence that Jesus survived the cross and lived to old age.[166] I make the case that Jesus never died on the cross in my book, *The Mobbing of Jesus Christ.* If that is indeed the case, then it wasn't the spirit of Jesus who gave the writings contained in the Book of Revelation to his disciple, John. It was Jesus himself in his attempt to warn the churches, and us, about the fraud being perpetrated by the impostors who call themselves apostles but are not. [See Revelation 2:2].

The Book of Revelation opens with the following prologue:

"The revelation from Jesus Christ, which God gave him to show his servants what must soon take place. He made it known by sending his angel to his servant John, who testifies to everything he saw - that is, the word of God and the testimony of Jesus Christ. Blessed is the one who reads aloud the words of this prophecy, and blessed are those who hear it and take to heart what is written in it, because the time is near.[167]

It was not an angel who relayed Revelation to John. It was Jesus himself in an attempt to put the genie back in the bottle. However, it is as impossible to put genies back in bottles as it is to correct the record without providing complete and utter truth. We cannot be vague and skirt around truth if we ever hope to reclaim stolen legacies and history – particularly when anything other than truth (illusion) can always be manipulated by people with power and control over the information.

From the time it was written, people have been interpreting Revelation's very symbolic and esoteric message as an end times message. I would say it is an end times message but not an end of world message. It is an attempt to reclaim the message from the impostor apostle in the form of the self-named Apostle Paul. However, the text is so clouded in symbology and mystery that it is almost incomprehensible, and that has left it open to so much interpretation that it is almost useless. However, what is not incomprehensible in the text are the letters to the seven churches, all of which we know were founded by Paul.

What follows are seven letters to the churches of Ephesus, Smyrna, Pergamum, Thyatira, Sardis, Philadelphia and Laodicea contained in Revelation 2-3. All these letters are similar in that they are basically saying that the churches have been invaded by false teachings. Here are some excerpts from those letters:

> **To Ephesus**: "I know that you cannot tolerate wicked people, that you have tested those who claim to be apostles but are not, and have found them false."

> **To Smyrna**: "I know your afflictions and your poverty—yet you are rich! I know about the slander of those who say they are Jews and are not, but are a synagogue of Satan."

> **To Pergamum**: "There are some among you who hold to the teaching of Balaam, who taught Balak to entice the Israelites to sin so that they ate food sacrificed to idols and committed sexual immorality. Likewise, you also have those who hold to the teaching of the Nicolaitans. Repent therefore!"

> **To Thyatira**: "I know your deeds, your love and faith, your service and perseverance, and that you are now doing more

than you did at first. Nevertheless, I have this against you: You tolerate that woman Jezebel, who calls herself a prophet. By her teaching she misleads my servants into sexual immorality and the eating of food sacrificed to idols."

To Sardis: "These are the words of him who holds the seven spirits of God and the seven stars. I know your deeds; you have a reputation of being alive, but you are dead. Wake up! Strengthen what remains and is about to die, for I have found your deeds unfinished in the sight of my God."

To Philadelphia: "I will make those who are of the synagogue of Satan, who claim to be Jews though they are not, but are liars—I will make them come and fall down at your feet and acknowledge that I have loved you. Since you have kept my command to endure patiently, I will also keep you from the hour of trial that is going to come on the whole world to test the inhabitants of the earth."

To Laodicea: "I know your deeds, that you are neither cold nor hot. I wish you were either one or the other! So, because you are lukewarm—neither hot nor cold—I am about to spit you out of my mouth. You say, 'I am rich; I have acquired wealth and do not need a thing.' But you do not realize that you are wretched, pitiful, poor, blind and naked. I counsel you to buy from me gold refined in the fire, so you can become rich; and white clothes to wear, so you can cover your shameful nakedness; and salve to put on your eyes, so you can see."

Jesus was sending this message to the very churches Paul founded. I cannot help but believe that among those *who claim to be apostles but are not* that Jesus warned the Ephesians about is the self-named apostle Paul. Also, Paul fits the bill for being one of those who say they are Jews and are not. I always found it curious that Paul was meeting with the temple priests in Jerusalem while trying to convert the rest of the world to a foreign form of Judaism to which no Jew adhered, most of all Jesus. Paul significantly changed and manipulated every scripture he ever quoted in order to make it fit into a doctrine that was attractive, nonrestrictive and easy to follow for all the gentiles he wanted to bring into his churches.[168]

If the message Jesus sent to these seven churches in any way applies to modern-day churches, then it is because those churches continue to focus on the books of the New Testament authored by Paul over the four Gospels of Jesus. No servant can serve two masters. He will either hate one and love the other or be devoted to one and despise the other. The teachings of Jesus and Paul are inconsistent with one another. It is up to us to decide which one to believe …and not to believe if we so wish.

Jesus tells us we are the source of our own salvation. Paul tells us that salvation comes from saying we believe that Jesus Christ died and was raised from the dead for the forgiveness of our sins. I know which man provided me with the teachings that helped heal my mind during the darkest time of my life and which man kept me from those teachings for so many years when they would have protected me from the darkness.

I think we must rid our minds of the concept implanted in us by Christianity that destroying a righteous and good human being was God's way of saving humanity. That doctrine falls under the same irrational mindset as that held by Hitler and Caiaphas and must be eradicated from our thinking as the delusion that it is. The God of creation would never kill its own creation to save it. That makes no logical sense. It is a human doctrine arising from a very human mindset that believes the greatest sacrifice one could ever make would be the sacrifice of one's child. It is the theology of those who believe in a guy-in-the-sky God that Jesus spent his life trying to eradicate with his teachings on the I AM of consciousness. In fact, it got him in trouble on more than one occasion when the Pharisees accused him of equating himself to God because they were all guy-in-the-sky believers.

The doctrine of one man's death for one man's sin as a means of saving humanity was just part of a huge misdirection campaign authored by Saul/Paul. Paul's misdirection killed two birds with one stone. It changed the message and thereby kept the power and control in the hands of the Pharisees as Caiaphas originally wanted with his attempted killing of Jesus. It also tied the hands of the apostles of Jesus. They couldn't counter Paul's false message without giving credence to Caiaphas' claim that Jesus was indeed an impostor. I believe a deal was thereby struck between the Apostle Peter and Paul that Paul would preach his false message to the gentiles and that Peter and the other eleven disciples would continue to preach to the Jews. It was a fateful deal that has had unbelievable consequences for humanity as a whole.

Jesus is not the Messiah because he died for our sins, as Paul taught. He is the Messiah because he showed us the way back into the Garden of Eden through the fiery sword with more clarity than any prophet or person before or after him. He gave us the means for making Earth our heavenly home while we are here and before we return to our actual home after death of the physical body. It has taken over two thousand years for his teachings and knowledge of how the human mind works to filter into our consciousness through new age beliefs, cognitive and behavioral psychology and the discovery of ancient texts like the Nag Hammadi library and Dead Sea Scrolls.[169] These texts are considered heretical by the Christian church, yet they reaffirm the New Testament teachings of Jesus.

The reason the texts are deemed heretical is because Christianity has chosen to focus on the 'heretical' teachings of the self-appointed apostle Paul. They chose Paul because his teachings are what built the churches by giving the non-Jewish gentiles an easy way to salvation without having to sacrifice any of the patterns of thought that Jesus said need to be sacrificed in order to repent and turn back to the original programming of the Creator. That is all repentance is. It is a turning back to our natural state of reality and truth. In the allegory of Adam and Eve, they are unable to repent when faced with the truth that appears in the form of God.

Jesus provided us with truth and that is why he was killed. Truth is hard when the illusion has taken hold of an environment or society, as it had the Pharisaic community of Jesus' day. What Paul did was create his own illusory environment in his churches by creating the lie that salvation comes with a simple declaration that one believes that Jesus died for the sins of humanity. An eye for an eye. A tooth for a tooth. A man for a man. Jesus' death for Adam's sin. That was the logic Paul used to create his empire of churches.

Although Peter taught it as well, the idea that an external holy Spirit enters your body upon a declaration that you believe in the resurrected Christ really took hold in the gentile churches of Paul because he was the only authority they could turn to. They were not Jews. They did not have any of the background the Jews had for understanding Jesus and his message. They were blank slates upon which Saul/Paul could write any message he wanted. And he did. He created his own doctrine that had no resemblance to the teachings of Jesus.

Paul had an agenda. He was a Pharisee educated in the law under Gamaliel and would have known the Old Testament scriptures inside and out, just as Jesus did, yet I challenge anyone to provide me with a single Old Testament scripture or story that Paul accurately quoted. They will not be able to do it because he misquotes them every time in his letters. An accurate accounting of those scriptures never left his mouth and that is because he needed to rephrase everything to fit his doctrine.

It was Paul's doctrine, without all the burdensome rituals and laws, that became Christianity when it was accepted by the gentiles. Just a declaration and some grace will absolve you of all your sins and get you into heaven. The hard work of self-awareness and self-examination that was the cornerstone of Jesus' message was altogether lost in Paul's mythos. This teaching has caused an entire generation to reject it in this age of reason and technology because on its face, it has no lasting effect on the character of the person who accepts it. How can a holy Spirit, or spirit of any kind for that matter, change who we are when we ourselves are the drivers of our lives and destinies? By accepting the myth, we turn our personal power over to something that has never existed in the first place.

There is a wonderful opportunity for the church here. As psychologists and psychiatrists get lazier and greedier in this illusory world and prescribe pills in place of ongoing therapy, the church can help fill the void. But first the doctrine needs to be put in line with the reality of Jesus' message. No longer can the Church take the easy road and say all people are saved by the sacrifice of Jesus. They need to accept and teach the message of unforgiven sin. That is how people will come alive spiritually – by knowing how their minds work and no longer allowing the responsibility for wrong thought patterns and behavior to be placed on an illusory devil outside themselves that fights with a false holy Spirit within. It is not a burden to shoulder this responsibility. It is freedom – absolute and joyous freedom knowing we can direct our lives in a way that brings us personal order and peace in a chaotic and depressing world. It cuts through all the confusion of an unexamined life. Mistakes are minimized and thereby there are few regrets. Surprisingly, money takes on less significance because it is a currency that was created in the illusion. A simple life becomes a preferable option to one of debt and trying to keep up with the neighbors.

We have ears but if you are like me when I was attending church as a child and young adult, you have never listened to Jesus. We have relied on the experts in the Church to tell us what the truth is instead of finding out for ourselves. Jesus's central message is that our thoughts determine our character because they lead us to the choices we make in our lives. This idea is not new age thought. It is Jesus translating the Jewish scriptures in the way they were meant to be translated for purposes of helping the human condition.

Why do we want to accept another man's interpretation of Jesus' teachings as gospel when we have the words of the master himself? I have pretty much limited my study of the New Testament to the gospels of Matthew, Mark, Luke and John – the four gospels of Jesus. Those four gospels, along with the Gnostic texts that the Christian Church condemned as heresy, provide us with all we need to know about Jesus, his teachings and the experiences he had with the Pharisees who threw him off his desired path and opened the door for the false teachings of the impostor apostle named Paul. I write about all of this extensively in my other books and won't expand upon it here except to say that Jesus's teachings about truth and illusion [good and evil] were as novel to the people then as they are to us now because the institution of religion got in the way.

I think we get caught up in the verbiage of sin, evil, hell, Satan and all the rest of it. It all sounds so frightening, like something out of the Exorcist. We need to remember these are just words that Jesus and the Bible used to express concepts and life lessons each of us needs to learn if we are to ever live in an orderly universe with one another. When we prescribe moralistic tones to the words, which they were never meant to have, they completely lose their meaning. That's largely why Jesus has become irrelevant to our lives and his message a joke to many people.

The church has handed God's work over to psychologists and psychiatrists, but they can only provide help after the fact, just as all our laws are only band aids on the actual wound. They cannot prevent this bad behavior in the first place. Only an understanding of spiritual laws and universal principles and a knowledge of the consequences for acting in opposition to them can do that.

Jesus' teachings are just now being used in modern behavioral, cognitive and exposure therapies because his philosophy is a philosophy of the mind – what religion refers to as the soul. When understood and applied properly, his teachings have the ability to take our consciousness to the next level in the evolutionary cycle. As it is, we are living in the 21st century world with a 1st century consciousness. Jesus could have taken us to the next level over 2,000 years ago but the teachings got lost in favor of worshiping the man himself.

Interpreting John 3:16 In Light Of Jesus' Own Words

In John, Chapter 3, Jesus is having a conversation with Nicodemus. Nicodemus is described as a ruler of the Jews in the first verse of the chapter, but he claims to know nothing of the spirit that Jesus always spoke about. Jesus tells him that no one has gone up to heaven except the one who has come down from heaven. It all goes back to Genesis 1:27, which says that mankind is made in the image of God on the sixth day of creation.

Jesus then tells Nicodemus that God so loved the world that he gave his only Son, so that everyone who believes in him will not perish, but instead, have everlasting life. Now, compare that statement with the one in Genesis 2:5, where it says that after God had rested on the seventh day he decided to make a physical structure in which the Man he created on the sixth day could inhabit here on earth. This was done in order that there be a physical structure to take care of the physical creation. This is the differentiation between physical man (flesh made on the eighth day) and spiritual man (human consciousness made in the image of God on the sixth day). The physical man does not become spirit until God breathes the breath of life into him in verse 7. Life is the spiritual man and flesh has no life outside the spirit.

The Book of Genesis then goes on to say that the Lord God planted a garden Eden, in the east, and placed there the man whom he had formed. Metaphysically, the word 'east' means within and the word 'Eden' allegorically represents "the elemental life and intelligence placed at the disposal of man and through which he is to evolve both mind and body. The human body with its psychical and spiritual attributes comprises a miniature Garden of Eden."[170]

This is why Jesus told Nicodemus no one has gone up to heaven except the one who has come down from heaven and what is born of flesh is flesh and what is born of spirit is spirit. He then utters the famous verse that is always used by Christians to claim Jesus is the only son of God:

> "For God so loved the world that he gave his only begotten son that whosoever believeth in him should not perish but have everlasting life." John 3:16

The way this verse is worded, it sounds like commentary from a scripture writer who is talking about Jesus' purpose on earth. Once I actually began reading the Bible I was surprised to learn that these words were actually spoken by Jesus himself. A Christian might argue that Jesus knew all along it was his mission to die on the cross for our sins and that is why he uttered these words. However, when interpreted in the context of the entire chapter within which it is written, one cannot help but conclude that Jesus is not referring to himself as God's only begotten Son – he is referring to all human beings as the sons and daughters of God.

Being the master illusionist he was, the impostor apostle Paul took this foundational teaching of Jesus and turned it completely upside-down. In I Corinthians 15:46, Paul writes the following:

> The first man, Adam, became a living being. The last Adam a life-giving spirit. But the spiritual was not first; rather the natural and then the spiritual. The first man was from the earth, earthly; the second man, from heaven. As was the earthly one, so also are the earthly, and as is the heavenly one, so also are the heavenly.

This is how heaven got separated from earth and became a place we go to when we die if we earn it through our actions. During the worst depression of my life, Paul's teachings are the reason I kept feeling like I wanted to go home not knowing where home was or how to get there.

Jesus was leading us home. He was showing us the way to get through the fiery sword placed at the gates of the Garden of Eden. Paul and his cohorts couldn't have that. They had to steer us in the opposite direction. What better way to do that than to distort the truth wherever and whenever you can? Paul was telling his gentile church followers that they were children of the earth. They were meant to eat the dust of the land. He was putting them outside the Garden and telling them it was their natural state of being. Paul is the one who tells us we are born in sin and we cannot get out of it until we declare Christ as our savior. But how can we declare Christ as our savior while believing the opposite of what he showed us? It is a worthless declaration based on a lie told to us by a man who has been sanctified by a church who needs him to stay in business. Jesus told us as much in his letters to Paul's churches contained in Revelation but we refused to see what was right in front of our eyes. Maybe that is because the church has used the same strategies as the master illusionists to indoctrinate [propagandize] its followers so that their minds' programming stops at the level of the doctrine. Just try arguing the doctrine with a Christian and you will see what I mean. You will receive the same looks of incredulity that William Shirer received from the patrons of bars and cafes in Nazi Germany when he tried to debate them and they answered him with the bullet points of Goebbels' propaganda.

What Christianity did was to take John 3:16 and use it to separate out Jesus as the only son of God, in direct contradiction to what Genesis and Jesus himself tells us. Once they were able to make Jesus the only son of God, then the holy Spirit (our consciousness of good and evil) became an external spirit that comes to live in us only if we accept Jesus as our Lord and Savior. It put our salvation out of our own hands and placed it under the purview of a religious hierarchy, which is exactly where it needs to be to support all the workers that rely on this kind of salvation for their financial livelihoods. Preachers will repeat this verse over and over again to make the point that Jesus was sent to die for our sins. I suppose they are relying on the fact that they are preaching to people like me – someone who never bothered to read the Bible while going to church and instead relied on what my pastors and Sunday School teachers told me. Never once have I heard any of them clarify that these were the words of Jesus himself, much less explain why he said these words while he was still very much alive.

Jesus rose from the dead for sure, but he did it long before he uttered the words contained in John 3:16 and he did it the way anyone does it who is willing to truthfully confront the thoughts, beliefs, decisions and behaviors arising from an ego consciousness, which can be so contrary to those of an inborn consciousness of life, logic and truth. The early Christian church had a decision to make. It could concentrate on the awareness teachings of Jesus and use the example of Jesus to show us how to examine our own thoughts and motivations to make them clear of falsehoods, or it could focus on the man himself as the only son of God and use his resurrection from the dead to reinforce this version of events based in large part on this misinterpretation of John 3:16. It chose the latter because the last thing the leaders of the pack who ran the early church wanted was to give their followers the means of obtaining their own salvation. What would they need a church for then?

At the First Council of Nicaea convened by Roman Emperor Constantine in 325 AD, 318 bishops of the Catholic church came up with the Nicene Creed which officially recognized the Holy Trinity as three separate entities of God the Father, Jesus the Son of God and the Holy Ghost. They consciously chose the gospels and verses to include in the New Testament that reinforced their position and branded as heresy the other gospels that focused on Jesus' consciousness teachings.[33] With Jesus established as the only son of God, they had to interpret the rest of the Bible literally in order to present mankind as a sinful lot who needed the brand of salvation only the church could provide. They essentially did what the Pharisees did. They set themselves up as the gatekeepers to God and sent all their followers in the wrong direction. They told them to look outward for their mental health and well-being by making a shallow declaration that Jesus was their Lord and Savior, when all the while they should have been directing their followers to look within at their ego motivated minds just as Jesus did in the wilderness when he overcame his own ego by responding to its arguments and manipulations with the truth of who he was and what he wanted for his life. (See Matthew, Chapter 4)

The decisions the early church leaders made in the interest of their own egos has been a fateful one and it has put modern day church leaders in a very bad position. They sound silly to a mind of reason when they say that Jesus comes to live inside us when we confess our belief in him and they sound contradictory when they use the names of God and Jesus interchangeably to say the same thing. All this complexity and nonsense has played directly into the hands of the secular leaders of the pack who use it to make God look like a ridiculous concept with no place in a modern society.

Egos create saviors in order to create religions and Christianity was no different. Man-made saviors provide a religion's leaders with their own turf. This is the same kind of territoriality used in the animal kingdom arising out of our desire to hoard in order to survive. With the survival consciousness of ego, the goal is to hoard goods to protect against future loss. Without followers and the replenishment of followers from generation to generation, religious institutions are faced with the same dilemma that all institutions face when they rely on customers for their continued livelihood: how to stay relevant and avoid bankruptcy and/or dissolution. Religion is only as good as its doctrine. When you have a fanciful doctrine that is increasingly marginalized in an age of reason, a religion is bound to lose followers; particularly when many of that religion's leaders turn out to be hypocrites and criminals. Since religion is reliant on its followers for its monetary sustenance, there are few options available to it when its well-educated followers reject its implausible doctrine. Operating from the assumption that they cannot change the doctrine without destroying the religion, they turn to other means of stopping the bleeding like new branding that focuses on the more believable aspects of the doctrine, charismatic leadership and outright deceit by framing the Bible's message of personal prosperity through self-analysis into a physical message of material prosperity in an ego-conscious world. The church may be succeeding in attracting more followers with its very egocentrically conscious strategies, but their manipulations are on full display when one interprets Jesus' message of consciousness truthfully. To me, that makes their strategies far worse than the restrictive dos and don'ts of the Baptist church I grew up in because by employing these kinds of manipulations, the institution of Christianity is crossing over into the area of conscious evil that Jesus gave his life trying to free us from.

Chapter 10
Self-Analysis is the Lost Teaching of Jesus Intrinsic in the Concept of Sin That Cannot Be Forgiven

It is largely due to Christian teachings originating with Paul that we have come to think of good and evil in terms of morality. When we view ourselves as moral or immoral, human beings become very judgmental. Absolutely no one, not even criminals, wants to be thought of as bad people. We all want to think of ourselves as good people. That is why you will rarely hear criminals take responsibility for what they have done. More often than not, they claim it is the victim's fault in some way. They will say things like the victim shouldn't have dressed in a certain way; or they should have known better than to be in such a bad part of town after dark; or they deserve what they got after what they did to me. There are countless ways to rationalize bad behavior and unfortunately, most people are very creative in coming with them. The soldiers who found themselves in Allied detainment camps after the war wondered why they were being treated like criminals when in their minds they were just following orders like the good soldiers they believed themselves to be. Those soldiers fell victim to the same state of mind as the Pharisee leadership who harassed Jesus and sought his execution merely for speaking the truth; all the while thinking they were righteous men of God.

Although there are differences of degree, I think the majority of people think of themselves as good people. Most of us do not do any sort of regular self-analysis to figure out why we think we are good and whether there is any room for improvement because that kind of self-analysis does not come naturally. Looking at my own life's decisions realistically and honestly has been the most difficult process I have ever had to undertake and it has taken a good many years of daily study, research and self examination to come to the truth. I have had to create a mind that is completely clear of all rationalizations or justifications of one sort or another. Some are easy to spot and others, particularly those in conflict with the picture one has of oneself, are painful to acknowledge and destroy. However, this process must take place if one is to achieve a state of mind with the ability to remain constant through all the ups and downs of one's life without caving into the ever-increasing pressures of external environments founded on a false consciousness.

The Antichrist isn't a person. It is the mindset that allows us to think we are good people by using the rationalizations and false premises of an illusory false consciousness to control our thought processes and condone our wrong actions. It allows for the justification of any ideology or belief system no matter how irrational or malevolent. Jesus showed us how to identify and eradicate our illusory mindset and the wilderness journey serves as a sort of illustration for how to do it.

I believe the wilderness journey was indicative of the time in Jesus' life after he studied the law and when he could have become a Pharisee himself.[171] When Jesus was in the wilderness of a mind in conflict, he spent his time examining himself and reaffirming what he believed to be true. That's how Jesus was always able to think logically. His mind was balanced and bolstered by the wisdom he acquired from reading books and studying ancient scriptures, astronomy, philosophy, physics and metaphysics and medicine; as well as "other things, which the understanding of no creature had ever reached."[172]

The wilderness passage found in the Book of Matthew, chapter 4, reads as follows:

"Then Jesus was led by the Spirit into the desert to be tempted by the devil. He fasted for forty days and forty nights, and afterwards he was hungry. The tempter approached and said to him,"

Tempter: "If you are the Son of God, command that these stones become loaves of bread."

Jesus (Voice of Truth): "It is written: One does not live by bread alone, but by every word that comes forth from the mouth of God" (manna from Heaven).

Tempter: "If you are the Son of God, throw yourself down [from the parapet of the temple]. For it is written, He will command his angels concerning you, and with their hands they will support you, lest you dash your foot against a stone.

Jesus (Voice of Truth): "Again it is written, You shall not put the Lord, your God, to the test."

Then the devil took him up to a very high mountain, and showed him all the kingdoms of the world in their magnificence, and he said to him,

Tempter: "All these I shall give to you, if you will prostrate yourself and worship me."

Jesus (Voice of Truth): "Get away, Satan! It is written, The Lord, your God, shall you worship and him alone shall you serve."

Then the devil left him and, behold, angels came and ministered to him.

The only way to drive out all the negative and false thoughts, beliefs, rationalizations, feelings, emotions and desires we all have and hold is by analyzing them and replacing them with what we know to be the truth. This is the whole purpose of positive affirmations, of which Jesus was the originator. When he was in the wilderness, Jesus countered his own destructive thoughts with scriptures from the Bible. With every assertion the tempter makes, Jesus counters it with what he knows to be true from his study of the scriptures. I always picture Jesus as having a whiteboard and in one column he writes what his ego consciousness wants and in the other, he writes what he knows to be true in his own mind about himself. In the end, he goes with what will make him happy because it is in balance with his own mind and soul.

All of Jesus' messages are about being aware of what you are thinking, saying and doing at all times, so that you can avoid non-consciously doing the wrong thing before it is too late to change course. In Matthew 24:42-44, Jesus says to his disciples, "Stay awake! For you do not know on which day your Lord will come. Be sure of this: if the master of the house had known the hour of night when the thief was coming, he would have stayed awake and not let his house be broken into. So too, you also must be prepared, for at an hour you do not expect, the son of Man will come." In the Gospel of Thomas it reads as follows: "You are to be on your guard against the world. Arm yourselves with great strength, otherwise the robbers could find a way to come to you, and the difficulty which you expect will certainly materialize. Let there be among you a person with understanding."[173]

Jesus' warning to 'stay awake' is the very definition of awareness because it prevents a person from denying truth and begins opening their minds to how much truth has been corrupted by the falsehoods of doctrines, ideologies, groupthink, peer pressure, intimidation, rationalizations, justifications and all the other assaults on truth required for ego's very existence. It also warns us about human nature. I never knew what Jesus was talking about here until I began interpreting the Bible solely with regard to our mind and inner core.

Stripping away all the lies we tell ourselves and thereby revealing all the rationalizations and justifications we use to give ourselves permission to act in conflict with a consciousness of truth serves to reconnect us with our being – what Jesus called the Spirit of the Father within.

Jesus is the best example of someone who, for most of his life, retained a mind clear of the illusory ego. Jesus was never unbalanced in the way most of us are when we try to balance our false consciousness with our innate consciousness of the good and true. In certain circumstances, such as those the Nazi soldiers found themselves in, the ego consciousness wins out for purposes of personal survival within the hierarchy. For that reason, when you are operating within a hierarchy - as the vast majority of us are - it is very important to realize what you are willing and not willing to do within the confines of that hierarchy. Free will and free choice become limited when you have a boss telling you what to do.

Although it can be very difficult to retain a true consciousness as an environment descends into the illusion, it still can be done. Jesus tells us how when he says to the Pharisees, *"Every kingdom divided against itself will be laid waste, and no town or house divided against itself will stand. And if Satan drives out Satan, he is divided against himself; how, then, will his kingdom stand? But if it is by the Spirit of God that I drive out demons, then the kingdom of God has come upon you."* [Matthew 12:25]

In simplest terms, if God is the good and the true, then Satan is the not-good and the not true. If we want to retain a good and true consciousness, we must never fool ourselves into believing the not good is good and the not true is true. The only way I know how to do that is by gaining knowledge of the good and true and making sure we retain the good and true in our minds no matter what external environment we find ourselves in.

Knowledge of the good and true would have given the Nazi soldiers the courage they needed to face the truth of what they did to their fellow men and women while using the justification that they were just following orders and it would have prevented the Pharisees from using the laws of Moses to fleece and control the Jewish community they were entrusted with leading.

Equal In Consciousness (Under God)

Everything gets switched with a consciousness of truth. I believe that is what death is. I believe all people learn the truth of their existence and of how they lived their lives. All those who trampled the weak and defenseless in our society will face the consequences in a world directed by truth. Of course, the opportunity is available to everyone to obtain such a consciousness here on earth. Once they do, they will feel guilt over the way they treated others when they abused their power. From the bully at school to the politician who destroyed his opponent to win an election, the realization that they harmed the Spirit of another person for a pointless gain will knock them to their knees. When the truth hits them and they come to terms with the destructiveness their actions had on another human being, the guilt and remorse will be worse than any punishment another person could dole out for them. This is why rationalizations become so convenient for people who have done really bad things. They know instinctively it will hurt to face the truth of what they were capable of doing to another person. The unfortunate fact for them is that the truth cannot be avoided. They will have to face it either in this life or the next and it is always better to deal with a known quantity than an unknown one.

It was nothing other than arrogance for the Nazi leadership and soldiers to think that they could skirt around man made laws to protect themselves and not be held to account. They could turn their Jewish targets into sub-human cockroaches in their minds all they liked, but the truth still remains that they were human beings. All their falsehoods and character assassination cannot change that fact. As human beings, we are all connected to one another through our consciousness and that makes us equal to one another – without exception. Harm we inflict on another person breaks the connection and that connection must be repaired to retain an orderly universe. Man-made laws catch some violators and punish them, but spiritual laws catch all of us. We will be held to account for all our thoughts, choices and behavior. It is not about punishment. It is about order and balance.

The only reason we change our thinking from its natural state of logic and truth (reality) is to protect our self-interests in some manner or form. When we revert back to pure energy upon the death of our physical body and all the illusory structures we created in this finite world dissolve into space, we will then be subject to all the laws of energy without exception. If we refuse to live with a consciousness of truth while on this earth, then all the crimes against consciousness we commit while here will be addressed in the after life.

We will be made to understand the emotional and mental pain

we caused other people through our actions and words because learning and growth is the goal of a universe in constant change and flux. The illusory ego that protected us so well during our physical life will be non-existent. The curtain of ignorance will be pulled open and a person like Adolf Hitler will only have a consciousness of truth to reveal to him the personal pain and suffering he inflicted on every single person he harmed while operating through the ignorance of ego. The enormity of his suffering is almost too much to contemplate; however, the really daunting aspect of it is that it may be inevitable. It is not about a man in the sky judging us. It is about the inflexible, unchangeable, and immutable laws by which energy works to create order and balance in a vast and ever-changing universe. For every action, there is an equal and opposite reaction. The energy we used to nurture our egos in ignorance will be used to show us our consciousness of truth.

Our egocentric focus on the physical has caused us to think of this balance in terms of what some have labeled as karma, ie. the same energy used to hurt me will be used to hurt you kind of justice. This is the kind of justice a guy in the sky would dole out, but it has no relation to universal law and consciousness which can only be understood at the level of mind. I always liked believing that the pain in my life caused by other people would be experienced by them in kind, but on further thought, I do not think it works that way. We are each a universe unto ourselves. The balance is within each of us. It has to be. Some of those people who harmed my consciousness have no idea what they did to me. I had no idea about the pain I caused certain people in my life until I began to analyze myself truthfully. It is a very personal and individual experience. That is how each of us will experience our own awakening. It will not be a matter of others feeling the same pain they caused us. It will be a matter of each of us coming to understand that our actions caused pain. It is awareness. It is our own individual awareness. It is about acquiring understanding about our real nature as eternal consciousness. We will all come to it because it is reality. So in the end, it is not about karma or the tit for tat justice of ego. It is about individual awareness and awakening.

Chapter 11
Jesus and the Laws of Energy

One of my goals in writing this book is to ground the message of Jesus, in particular, in reality and truth where it belongs because it has been distorted over time by the Christian church with its heavy-handed use of the concepts of good and evil as opposing forces. I believe religion's concept of duality contained in the view of good and evil as opposing forces arose from the outward manifestation of thought as action, rather than from thought itself. Duality implies the existence of two [opposing] views. In reality, thoughts are neither good or evil, right or wrong. They are just streams of consciousness that result in actions we human beings have labeled as good and evil, right and wrong. Hence, we tend to view something as good or bad, right or wrong etc. However, it is not an either/or proposition. As the chart below illustrates, all is one: good and evil, right and wrong, depression and joy, ignorance and wisdom, and so on. They are all variants of the energy of our thoughts, rather than opposing states of mind.

CONSCIOUSNESS (MIND)
DIRECTS THE ENERGY OF OUR EMOTIONS AND
THOUGHTS IN A POSITIVE/NEGATIVE DIRECTION

Ego Consciousness   **Christ Consciousness**

Ego Consciousness		Christ Consciousness
Wrong	Good and evil, life and death, poverty and riches – all are from the Lord.	Right
Lawlessness		Righteousness
Enslavement		Freedom
Evil and devious	Sirach 11:14	Good and upright
Brutality		Mercy
Deception and Lies (Illusion)	(See Appendix II for other verses that	Truth (Reality)
Ignorance	support the view that God is both universal	Wisdom
Rigidity/Sternness	negative and positive energy)	Playfulness/Humor
Cowardice		Courage
Hate/Cruelty		Love/Compassion
Depression		Joy
Inner Turmoil		Inner Peace
Doubt and Fear		Faith and Courage
Pride		Humility

We carry all kinds of thoughts - - good and bad, positive and negative. They come and go in and out of our minds. They are energy at work. The energy of our thoughts is always in motion. The same amount of energy is exerted to create thoughts that we view as positive or right as is exerted in creating thoughts that we view as negative or wrong. As individual human minds, we are the sole determinants of how that energy gets directed and it is our responsibility to choose the thoughts we want to hold.

What I have concluded is that the energy of our thoughts is quite similar to energy manifesting in the physical world as hot and cold. Hot is not the opposite of cold. Rather, hot and cold are labels we give to variants in temperature. We can transform hot water to cold water by adding ice and cold water to hot by applying heat. Similarly, we can transform the energy of our thoughts so that our behavior results in actions that are labeled as hateful or loving, fearful or courageous, depressed or joyful, etc. If these thoughts were opposite, we would not be able to transform one into the other by focusing our mind (reason and emotion) in the direction we want it to go.

This ability to transform the energy of our emotions and thoughts from positive to negative and vice versa is our consciousness of good and evil or what is referred to in the Bible as the tree of the knowledge of good and evil and it is one force, not two opposing forces. At any moment in time, an individual is at different levels of consciousness in terms of thought. It is the concept of duality that has us thinking that the good and evil consciousness we have labeled as Satan and God are opposites. In actuality, Satan and God are labels we have given to variants of the life force I have labeled as 'consciousness' throughout this book.

One must understand this concept to understand this book. It was the concept Jesus was trying to convey when he said in Matthew 4:44-45, "But I say to you, love your enemies, and pray for those who persecute you, that you may be children of your heavenly Father, for he makes his sun rise on the bad and the good, causes rain to fall on the just and unjust." However, the view that good and evil are manifestations of one stream of consciousness labeled as God did not originate with Jesus. He got it from Old Testament scriptures that support the view that the consciousness of God controls the universal vibrations of positive and negative. (See Appendix 1 for some of these verses).

As conscious beings ourselves, we have the same ability to control the positive and negative vibrations of our thoughts. We create our internal existence through the creation of our thoughts and our external existence flows therefrom in the form of our words and actions.

At our core, we are energy created in the conscious form of God. One can call it the soul, the subconscious, the spirit or whatever; but it is, in reality, who we actually are. These 'garments of skin' that

God gives to Man and Woman before they are expelled from the Garden with their false consciousness, are not who we are.[174] Genesis 1:27 says, "God created mankind in his image in the image of God he created them; male and female he created them." According to this verse, Man and Woman are equally wrapped up in the mankind umbrella. There is no differentiation between them at the energetic level of their core being. Therefore, any differentiation made between them based on their physical gender, race, nationality or any other factor that differentiates them at the physical level are all part of the false (illusory) consciousness.

Consciousness is the one. It is the real and the true. However, the way it expresses through the brain in the form of our emotions and thoughts is what makes each of us unique. Creation itself is the output of a consciousness that wants to express itself in its creation. We create our existence every moment of our lives because we have control over the thoughts and feelings we choose to have. It can be a negative or positive existence based on those choices. We all have that power and no one and nothing outside of us can take that power from us. We can choose to give it over though and that is how our personal power is lost. We lose it to the illusion that someone else can take it from us.

When we talk about the human mind, the goal should always be to overcome the negative emotions and illogical thought patterns that create blockages and prevent us from living in the natural state of freedom and inner peace that comes when we are in alignment with the energetic consciousness of reality and truth. However, we should not make the mistake that so many religious and new age teachers make in believing that balance is a perfect mix. What I have found in all my research is that truth is an absolute. Honesty is an absolute. You cannot have balance between deception and truth, right and wrong. The goal should not be balance. It should be achieving equilibrium through counter-balance. We don't counter fear with a little bit of courage in order to find a balance between the two states of mind. We become courageous through the process of conquering fear. I believe the idea of balance being the goal has gotten confused with counter-balancing the negative with the positive as the method for achieving the goal and it belongs in the same category as the gray area of morality; ie. it is an illusion that should never have come into existence.

Jesus never intended his teachings to dictate behavior like our laws do. His focus was always on our being, rather than on our doing. All of his teachings are meant to work on the energy of our mind's emotions and thoughts. In order to interpret Jesus' message correctly, we must switch our perspective and then figure out how to make Jesus' message applicable to the energy of our consciousness, rather than to the physical behavior that results from the energy and choices of our consciousness.

One of the most interesting and provocative books on the question of evil is titled, *The Banality of Evil*, by Hannah Arendt. She was prompted to write it after attending the trial of Adolf Eichmann. She found him to be a very non-descript man who one would never picture as the murderer of millions of human beings. It prompted her to ask the question of whether one can do evil without being evil. Ultimately, she concluded that Eichmann was not a monster, but rather, that he performed evil acts due to the fact he became disengaged from the reality of his evil acts. He was acting with the thoughtlessness of a man who was unable to think from the standpoint of someone else. Lacking this empathetic characteristic trait allowed him to commit crimes with absolutely no idea about how wrong he was. In his own words, he was just trying to get on in life.

Jesus focused on our being, as did God in the Garden, by asking why questions, because if one focuses solely on the doing, it accomplishes little in terms of coming to grips with questions like the one Arendt grappled with. Should one even pose the question she posed? Does it really matter if one can be labeled evil or not evil if their outward behavior is in itself what one can clearly define with the label 'evil.' The fact that she concludes he was disengaged from the reality of his acts does not relieve him of responsibility for those acts. One could conclude all the soldiers who said they were just following orders were disengaged from the reality of their acts. One can say a man who kills his wife out of anger is disengaged from the reality of his evil act. One could even say that Hitler was disengaged from the reality of his evil acts. Disengagement itself is a quality of one's mind. Not being able to put oneself in a neighbor's shoes is a quality of one's mind.

I think Jesus himself answers Arendt's question in his address to the Church of Laodicea, found in the Book of Revelation, Chapter 3, verse 15 by saying, ""I know your deeds, that you are neither cold nor hot. I wish you were either one or the other! So, because you are lukewarm - neither hot nor cold - I am about to spit you out of my mouth" I would say the congregation at Laodicea is like the 80% of the population that I refer to in my book, *The Evolution of Good and Evil*, as the non-conscious because they are neither consciously good nor consciously evil. They just go along to get along without really ever undergoing any sort of self-evaluation to determine what is true and what is false within their own minds so that they can think, feel and act with awareness of that knowledge.

Jesus provides us with the method for doing that, which is allegorically represented as the method for getting through the fiery sword that God placed at the entrance of the Garden after throwing Adam and Eve out. Metaphysically, fire represents the self-examination that makes us identify and destroy the negative qualities that are keeping us from our own destiny.[175] Fire also represents the wisdom and courage we need to identify and call out the same negative qualities in other people so that they become powerless in their desire to harm us. Our metaphor for hell as fire is all wrong. Boiling water will always melt ice. Conformity is cold, barren and never changes. We need the fire of conscience in our minds to burn through all the remnants of our animal past and remind us that we are here to constantly change, grow, improve, find real solutions to problems so that we can move our evolution forward in a positive manner - grounded in the truth of equality for all through dignity and respect for each individual.

Based upon Eichmann telling the officer who arrested him that he was just trying to get on in life by doing what everyone else was doing when the officer asked him how he could have such concern for his own family while being responsible for the murder of millions of others; I would have to conclude that Eichmann was one of non-conscious. The same could be said for all the citizens, bureaucrats and soldiers who assisted in the holocaust by keeping their heads down so that they *could just get on in life*.[176]

It was Eichmann's responsibility to become aware during his time on this Earth. It was his responsibility to care for his own mind, even though it became very difficult to do that in Nazi Germany where one's livelihood was tied to being a bystander or enabler to the Nazi agenda.

As I study Nazi Germany, it gives me a great deal of understanding as to how difficult it is to keep one's mind grounded in truth when the external environment is set up to keep it in falsehood. It is easy to judge from a decades out view, but if we want to be truthful with ourselves, we need to put ourselves in the place of an Eichmann or a Nazi soldier and ask ourselves what we would have done in their place. Would we have moved out of Germany? Would we have quit our good-paying job as a bureaucrat within the regime to work in a cafe where no one's life was being taken, but wherein we could not support our family? Would we have defied the orders of our superiors and risked the dire consequences such action would have resulted in? As our neighbors were being taken away, would we have done anything on their behalf and risk being sent away ourselves?

I think the only way to prevent this corrupted inevitability is for each individual within the population to begin studying the laws of nature in terms of how they apply to the energy of our thoughts and emotions. These leaders of the pack are created, not born. Until the structures change through an organic change in our individual consciousness, we as individuals need to begin recognizing these human relics of a hierarchical, competitive, survival of the fittest kind of animal consciousness and refuse to let leaders of the pack like Hitler and Caiaphas manipulate the structures in order to reach the top rungs of our institutions.

Based upon what Hitler-led Germany has taught me, I would have to concur with Arendt that one can do evil without being evil. Perhaps we should quit using the term 'evil' altogether because, given certain circumstances, we are all capable of doing horrible things while under the illusion we are good people just trying to get along in life. I would contend we are all just individual human beings subject to inner and outer forces exerted upon our consciousness and I would argue that the moral connotations associated with the word 'evil' has prevented us from looking at ourselves and our world objectively and without judgment so that we can determine how best to create ways to optimize the energy of our consciousness so that it works for the benefit of the all (collective of individuals) without sacrificing the one (individual).

I believe Jesus' teachings are the best human template we have for showing us how to change, move, control, store and dissipate the energy of our emotions and thoughts in a manner that achieves balance in all aspects of our [core] being. Jesus and his teachings seem at odds with life today because our modern world is upside-down due to the false consciousness that we have carried over through centuries. Until we learn to live in a right side up world where the earth works for us and we work for the good of ourselves in the context of each other (Jesus' two greatest commandments) then Jesus will continue not to make sense to most people.

Universal Balance

Hitler's mind was wracked with feelings of hatred and revenge after he was unfairly thrown out into the street and back into poverty for expressing an unpopular opinion to his workmates. Instead of channeling his energy in a way that would dissipate and ultimately transform that negative energy into the positive flow of understanding, he sought out ways to seek his revenge using the same tactics his colleagues used against him. He fed Satan with Satan while always professing a belief in God throughout his destructive life. It was a totally egocentric, misguided and wrong view of God that reinforced his own destructive emotions and thoughts. However, Hitler is not the only person to have ever held this view. It is a view that many people hold. This God seeks its own revenge. It is the same God that Samuel believed in and that our authoritarian leaders believe in when they use the label of God to justify their wars. Quite frankly, it is the same God I sought out after a very unfair experience happened in my life. I would seek out Old Testament scriptures that reassured me the beasts who harmed me would be harmed in a similar way. It provided a release for all my own hatred and feelings of revenge. It is so hard to break free from that negative mindset because it has been ingrained in us for generation after generation. We need to feel it's true because our sense of fairness and justice is in the material plane where an eye for an eye and a tooth for a tooth seems reasonable and fair. It is the morality of a false ego consciousness that makes us believe we have to bestow justice ourselves if we are ever to obtain justice. It is a mindset that keeps us bitter, resentful, depressed and unable to adjust to the changing circumstances of life until we get our pound of flesh. It is limiting and destructive because it steals the peace of mind we should have in knowing that crimes against consciousness are covered by universal laws that will never fail. They can never be manipulated, changed or interpreted in favor of one party over another. They have only one interpretation that cannot be bought out, bribed, intimidated, pressured, deceived or settled by the human parties involved. The scales of the laws of cause and effect are always in balance because they are controlled by the laws of energy God uses to keep its universe in perfect equilibrium.

Chapter 12
Some Other Teachings of Jesus
Brought Within the Framework of Reality

1. Do Not Make a Vow - Let Your Yes Mean Yes, and Your No Mean No

Jesus warned in Matthew 5:33-34, "Again you have heard that it was said to your ancestors, 'Do not take a false oath, but make good to the Lord all that you vow. But I say to you, do not swear at all. Let your 'Yes' mean 'Yes,' and your 'No' mean 'No.' Anything more is from the evil one."

Most of us have sworn a vow at some point in our lives, whether it be to a club, friend, job, military or church. Vows are required when someone wants to create a sense of loyalty on the part of the person taking them. They are a part of the illusion because the only loyalty one should have in this world is our own loyalty to reality which is contained in our individual consciousness of the true and false.

As previously discussed, one of the first moves Hitler made after assuming power was to require the military to swear the following oath to him: "I swear by God this sacred oath, that I will render unconditional obedience to Adolf Hitler, the Fuehrer of the German Reich and people, Supreme Commander of the Armed Forces, and will be ready as a brave soldier to risk my life at any time for this oath." As William Shirer observed in his seminal work, *The Rise and Fall of the Third Reich*, this oath had dire consequences on the consciousness of the people who took it. The generals, who up until the time of taking the oath, could have overthrown the regime felt honor-bound to the person of Hitler after the oath. The oath also provided so many officers and soldiers with the rationalization they needed when faced with the truth of what they had done to their fellow men and women. Even further than that though, it gave them the delusional mindset that they were acting with honor while perpetrating the most horrible and degrading acts upon their fellow men and women. As Shirer writes, "By honoring their oath they dishonored themselves as human beings and trod in the mud the moral code of their corps."[177]

Along with serving as an open vow of loyalty, a vow can also serve as a form of deceit when the person taking it vows silence about wrongdoing they have seen or experienced. As testified to at Nuremberg, all the German sailors on the boat responsible for sinking the Athenia, a passenger liner on its way to America, were forced to sign a declaration that they would "keep secret all happenings of 3rd September, 1939, on board the U-30 submarine, from either foe or friend and erase from memory all happenings of that day."[178] Also, since vows are very effective in binding people to secrecy, they are commonly used in lawsuits that have settled to keep the accuser/plaintiff from voicing the harm that happened to them at the hands of the defendant(s).

However, when Jesus warned us to never swear a vow, I think he may have been emphasizing the kind of oath we make to ourselves rather than someone else. This kind of oath is destructive because it is usually made to get an outcome the individual making it personally desires. For example, a person may pray something along the lines of, 'Lord if you make my father well, I will begin going to church' or 'Lord, if you save me from this fate, I will begin doing what's right.' By making these types of vows or promises, we put qualifications on when we will serve our own consciousness of true and false. There should never be qualifications of this sort, as we should be serving it every single moment of our lives. Even in taking a vow of priesthood or a vow to accept Jesus as our savior, we are putting qualifications on how we choose to think. For example, Christianity would not approve of my views on salvation and forgiveness, but I have chosen to follow the teachings of Jesus as I understand them from my studies and research. Tao, Buddhism and new age philosophies opened my eyes to what I believe is the truth of what Jesus taught. If I had followed church doctrine and closed my mind to other ideas, I would never have arrived at a philosophy that helps me live a life in keeping with the calling of my own soul and brings me the most peace.

As the Nazi military did, we feel obligated to uphold our vows and have a sense of guilt when we break them. That is exactly the reason why we should never make them if we want to continue our own personal growth and knowledge. Oaths limit our knowledge base and stilt the evolution of our eternal consciousness. Food energizes the body and knowledge energizes and expands the mind. Nothing should be left off the table when it comes to learning and introducing ourselves to new experiences and different points of view.

Jesus makes clear in the Book of John that the holy spirit is not a third entity that enters the body at the calling of his name. He tells his disciples in John 14:15-20 that the advocate he is sending them is "the Spirit of Truth, which the world cannot accept because it neither sees nor knows it. But you know it, because it remains with you and will be in you and when he comes, the Spirit of truth will guide you to all truth."[179]

Truth - the God in the Garden of Eden, the holy spirit that came down in the form of a dove after Jesus was baptized and the only holy spirit Jesus was talking about when he said he would send it to his disciples after his death - is separate and apart from morality, religious doctrines, political ideologies, cultural mores, national allegiances and group identification; all of which are founded on a false assumption because they all promote a group experience and belief. Our individual experiences and upbringing are unique, therefore, only the individual consciousness can root out and change all the false premises of thought it has acquired over a lifetime. The process of separating the chaff from the wheat as Jesus put it can only be done at the level of the individual. Laws cannot do it, schools cannot do it, workplaces cannot do it. We must do it for ourselves based on some basic premises of reality, the most important of which is that we are all equal at the level of energy. The fact that we are equal does not mean that we are the same. Sameness is a manifestation of ego that tries to put groups of us in boxes to which we are expected to conform or suffer the consequences for stepping out. Equality is the recognition that the consciousness of Creation expresses in an infinite number of ways and wants to express through each one of us individually to create the masterful paradise on earth it imagines. That is the foundational truth upon which we should begin our personal self-anlysis to start building a framework for how we choose to interact with our external environments. It is only by resisting conformity and having the courage to be truthful with ourselves about all aspects of 'our self' that we will be able to break free of the structures that box us into predefined lives that take us off course from our destiny in truth and reality.

Jesus' philosophy requires us to be individual islands of mind because the illusory consciousness (a/k/a ego consciousness) separates us. We must never lose sight of our existence as eternal, conscious beings, but we must fight for that consciousness on the battlefield of ego. We must create a value system that nurtures the trinity nature of our consciousness, while at the same time, acquire a realistic knowledge of ego.

I think many of the people targeted by the Nazi regime had no idea about how a community of people they knew and trusted could turn so vicious and cruel. It left them unprepared in confronting the reality of the situation and taking steps that would have protected them emotionally, mentally, physically and financially. It would have required them to make heart-wrenchingly difficult decisions that, quite frankly, the majority of us would be unable to make. In such situations, stasis seems preferable to most of us while we wait for someone to come along who will stop the madness and save us. Unfortunately, in an environment where the illusion has become the reality, there is usually no one left who fits the bill as savior because they have been killed, incarcerated, silenced, banished or otherwise neutralized.

Additionally, it must be acknowledged that proactive measures to protect our consciousness are easy when it is an individual or a few individuals assaulting it. It becomes much harder when an entire society has turned against the truth in favor of the illusion. In order to protect our house before the robbers come, as Jesus warned us, we must ask ourselves some questions ahead of time. How hard will we be willing to fight? How far will we go to protect ourselves? Will we stay the course in acting in accordance with what we know is true, or will we submit in order to survive? As you can understand, it becomes quite a different playing field when an entire group, environment or society has turned against you. You must prepare yourself ahead of time by understanding the true nature of your reality here on earth instead, of denying it and hoping that there will always be someone to come to your rescue because the reality is that there may come a time in your life when the only rescuer is yourself.

Christianity has turned this utterly false and destructive mindset of salvation into dogma by preaching that Jesus will return to save his flock when the illusion overtakes the world. The reality is that Jesus was here and he lived and breathed his entire life in an illusory environment. He taught us how to prepare our minds so that they do not fall victim to a state of stasis when the group comes for us individually. It would be wise for all Christians to stop believing in Jesus' return to save them and to instead heed his words, "If you have ears, hear!"

2. Do Unto Others As You Would Have Done to You and Love Your Enemies

In cases of extreme harm done to an individual, it is so easy to lose sight that the same consciousness inhabits the bodies of both the wrongdoer and the wronged. Our human reaction, more often than not, is to want revenge in order to get our pound of flesh. However, I do not think that is the natural reaction of a person who knows the nature of human consciousness. I remember reading a story of a lawyer who was defending a drunk driver who killed his best friend in an accident that happened while the defendant was drunk. The lawyer argued that if he had been in the position of the friend who was killed, he would not want the driver (his best friend) to go to jail for manslaughter. He was crucified for it but I believe the reason he felt that way is that he would not want his friend to suffer like that. Period. There are cases where family members have made the same kind of statement when a child has killed a parent. They know the mother and/or father would not want the child to go to prison. In the case of a stranger brutally killing a family member, the empathy does not run so deep. However, letting our judgment and feelings turn them into monsters undeserving of basic human dignity because of what they did has turned many of us into the same kind of savages we detest. It is certainly what happened to Hitler when he became the same kind of person as the work colleagues he detested. Satan cannot drive out Satan. The same kind of energy applied to the most gruesome and detestable killers and rapists in our society will not rehabilitate them. It will just feed their already totally corrupted consciousness and reinforce in their minds that what they did was natural and okay because it is being done to them.

When Jesus said do unto others as you would have done to you, he did not intend for you to apply it to situations and people where it is easy. It is meant to be done in those situations where it is the absolute last thing you would ever consider doing. When a person is severely harmed at the hands of another person, it is extremely hard to understand, much less sympathize, with the perpetrator(s) of the harm. However, isn't that exactly what Jesus did on the cross when he said, "Forgive them Father for they know not what they do." Christ knew that the people who crucified him were acting in ignorance of what true sin and evil is. As he had told them, "Before me, there was no sin. But now you have no excuse for your sin." People who say only God can forgive sin are wrong. The God within us can make us capable of forgiving the most horrific acts committed against us and our loved ones. It is not easy, and it takes a ton of self-work and learning to understand why they hurt us, but it can be done. It was because of Jesus' divine nature that he was capable of interceding on his killers' behalf, even as the crime was being committed.

The Christian church has interpreted Jesus' intercession on his killers' behalf as an intercession for all of humanity. By doing so, they have taken away all the power of his divine understanding of how the human mind works. He knew the council had already rationalized their actions and the individuals in the mob were incapable of taking personal responsibility for their actions. His request to forgive them for they know not what they do repaired the break in consciousness and brought forth the balance that was lost through their actions. His compassion is unfathomable, but it is a quality we should all be working towards as the conscious creators of our reality here on earth.

3. The Meek Shall Inherit the Earth

We have misinterpreted what it means to be meek, just as we have misinterpreted much of what Jesus wanted us to know. The Bible was originally written in Greek and Latin, and then translated into English. In the process of going from language to language, the nuances of many words in the original text got lost in translation. In the original Greek text, the word for meek is "praus", which means to gain control over something without taking away any of its strength. An example of praus would be when a wild horse is tamed. The horse retains the power and strength in its legs after taming, but it is controlled strength which allows a person to ride it.[180]

Translating praus as meek, is almost the equivalent of saying that east means west. They are polar opposites in meaning. This mistranslation has completely distorted what Jesus means in the Sermon on the Mount, when he says that the meek are blessed and will inherit the earth. It has also spawned a generation of people who think that being a Christian means that they have to maintain a mild and subdued manner towards other people to appear holy. Jesus was not instructing us about our attitude towards other people. He was telling us that we should seek guidance from the divine power within us and make ourselves obedient to it, so that we can have power over the emotions and thoughts generated by our minds.

Jesus himself was anything but mild and subdued. He was larger than life. His character traits were a huge part of why his message resonated so well with his audiences. He was not only speaking with the force and power of truth behind him, he was living (being) that way. He would have been horrified, and quite possibly angered, by the false sweetness and goodness of so many people who have misinterpreted his message.

Jesus told his disciples that he came to bring fire upon the world. Those don't sound like the words of a man who wants us to be mild and unassuming. Quite the contrary. He wanted us to achieve our destiny and purpose on earth by being fully conscious of the divine spirit within us (the holy Spirit). This is what he meant when he said the meek would inherit the earth.

4. Appearances

Jesus passionately denounced the Pharisees' manipulation of outward appearances to make themselves feel righteous and superior telling his audience in Matthew 23 how everything they did was done to be seen by others. To Jesus, the real and true aspect of a human being was the part that was unseen – what he called the spirit of the Father within. He told the Pharisees they were like whitewashed tombs, which appear beautiful on the outside, but inside are full of dead men's bones and every kind of filth: "On the outside you appear righteous, but inside you are filled with hypocrisy and evildoing."[181]

For Jesus, the only real part of himself was his mind and ideas. He was punished by the Pharisees for openly and honestly expressing those ideas. In other words, he was punished for being who he was because in an egoistic environment where reputations are what is real, his ideas hurt the image of the religious hierarchy of Pharisees who were using their job titles and positions to define themselves to the world. When you read his interactions with them in the Gospels of Matthew, Mark, Luke and John, Jesus was constantly leaving them speechless. They were speechless because they were incapable of bravely expressing their own ideas to him knowing that if they did, they knew they would be putting the illusion they created at risk. Instead, they lied about him and did everything they could to destroy his character by calling him a drunkard and glutton before they were finally able to arrest him on false charges of blasphemy.[182]

Jesus said of the Pharisees, "Beware of false prophets, who come to you in sheep's clothing, but underneath are ravenous wolves. By their fruits you will know them. Do people pick grapes from thorn bushes, or figs from thistles? Just so, every good tree bears good fruit, and a rotten tree bears bad fruit. A good tree cannot bear bad fruit, nor can a rotten tree bear good fruit. Every tree that does not bear good fruit will be cut down and thrown into the fire. So by their fruits you will know them."

A corrupt mind hides itself wherever it can. Adam and Eve hid in the bushes. We always hear about the spouse abuser who family and friends refuse to believe is capable of such violence. Or the mild-mannered church deacon who abuses children and the church stands behind him because they cannot believe it. Or the kid who shoots the cashier at a local 7-11 and whose parents and teachers swear up and down what a good kid he is and would never intentionally hurt anyone. Corruption needs to operate in a false environment in order to achieve its goals. Jesus warns us not to be easily taken in. We need to be able to recognize these kinds of people to defend ourselves and our souls. The flip side is also true. We cannot assume if someone is different in appearance or manner from what we deem to be "normal", that they are evil.

Although the Jews were the most outwardly traumatized group due to Hitler's mindset put into action, the entire country and the countries he conquered were traumatized as well. And judging by the way the Nazi soldiers and commanders denied their roles, passed responsibility on to others and committed suicide at the end of the war; the case can be made that they were the most inwardly traumatized group of all because their actions inflicted the most harm on their fellow men and women while their minds were corrupted by the false ideology. When forced to face truth, which the Nuremberg trials certainly did, it is no surprise that they wore sunglasses, looked down, tried to hide behind their false shows of boredom, made denials, justifications, rationalizations, feigned forgetfulness, and played the blame game – all to keep the spotlight of truth from shining upon them and making them face the facts that it was their own words and actions (not Hitler's) that inflicted so much pain and damage on their fellow men and women.

However, one shouldn't think they are out of the woods by escaping accountability in this life. Each and everyone of us arc destined to have the spotlight of truth shone upon us. Hitler's henchmen and goons who caused so much destruction to the collective soul of humanity, all considered themselves to be good family men and women. They hid behind their beautiful families, I believe, as a means of trying to protect their own souls. It made them feel like they were good men and women since they were such good mothers and fathers. However, all the rationalizations, justifications, lies and false appearances created by an ego consciousness that fool us into believing we are good, as our thoughts and behavior indicate otherwise, are like dust in the wind. They are illusions that count for nothing when Truth comes walking through the Garden. Being a good husband and father, or good wife and mother will only take you so far. Truth does not compartmentalize our actions and roles as we like to do. Truth sees all and understands all. Science has shown us that for every action there is an equal and opposite reaction and Jesus said it in his own way when he said in Matthew 5:18 that "until heaven and earth pass away, not the smallest letter or the smallest part of a letter will pass from the law." He was not talking about Mosaic law. He was talking about universal law by which we are all bound regardless of religion or beliefs. Whether we want to face reality or not, the fact remains that in this life or the next, we will all be held to account for violations against our own consciousness and the consciousness of those around us. It is simply the nature of reality.

The End

POSTSCRIPT

In writing this book and after having written my other books on Jesus and human consciousness, I have come to the realization that we will always have to deal with the Bully-Enabler-Bystander-Target model of thought and behavior that I describe in my book, *The Evolution of Good and Evil*. It is the framework upon which existence has been built on this earthly plane. Although I cannot say why it was constructed that way, the Garden of Eden allegory provides some hope that this earthly plane can be rebuilt upon systems that nourish and sustain all life in a more positive environment which provides for the needs of all without diminishing the needs of the one (individual). As I view the allegory now, it is a vision of the future rather than a story of the past.

There is no more time to hide from the truth of our existence. Once the reason for our existence is made clear as Jesus wanted it made, the pointlessness of living in illusion will be revealed. Everything, without exception, will be affected when we begin turning our consciousness right side up. All the beliefs and patterns of thought and behavior we built our lives on before will begin to look ridiculous. As the false consciousness is dissolved, so also will go all the anxiety, depression, joylessness, sense of unfulfillment, grief and restlessness that currently defines the lives of many, if not most of us, and which we take for granted as just being the reality of life on planet earth.

Jesus said to the Pharisees, "The stone that the builders rejected has become the cornerstone; by the Lord has this been done, and it is wonderful in our eyes. Therefore, I say to you, the kingdom of God will be taken away from you and given to a people that will produce its fruit."

In my eyes, the stone the builders rejected is the same stone

Eve rejected when she ate the fruit. It is our natural human ability to determine what is false and what is true (our Holy Spirit/Kingdom of the Father within) and stick to what is true with the faith that it will take us to where we need to be.

This will be my last book. From here on out, I am going to narrow my focus on nourishing my own growth and internal prosperity as well as support the growth and internal prosperity of those around me. That will be my own contribution to the attainment of humanity's birthright in this earthly Garden of Eden. Godspeed to us all and God's blessings on us all!

APPENDIX I

SPIRIT IS ETERNAL AND MOVES IN EITHER DIRECTION AS OUR CONSCIOUSNESS DIRECTS IT – EVEN AFTER DEATH

The Old Testament does not use the word "Satan." All evil and good come from the same Consciousness which the Old Testament calls Yahweh or God.

Know then, that the LORD, your God, is God: the faithful God who keeps covenant mercy to the thousandth generation toward those who love him and keep his commandments, but who repays with destruction those who hate him; he does not delay with those who hate him, but makes them pay for it. Therefore carefully observe the commandment, the statutes and the ordinances which I command you today.

Deuteronomy 7:9-11

See, I set before you this day a blessing and a curse; a blessing for obeying the commandments of the LORD, your God, (doing the right thing) which I give you today; a curse if you do not obey the commandments of the LORD, our God, but turn aside from the way I command you today, to go after other gods (money, power, fame) whom you do not know.

Deuteronomy 11:26-28

On a good day enjoy good things, and on an evil day consider; both the one and the other God has made, so that no one may find the least fault with him.

Ecclesiastes 7:14

Everything is the same for everybody; the same lot for the just and the wicked, for the good, for the clean and the unclean, for the one who offers sacrifice and the one who does not. As it is for the good so it is for the sinner; as it is for the one who takes an oath, so it is for the one who fears an oath. Among all the things that are done under the sun, this is the worst, that there is one lot for all. Hence the hearts of human beings are filled with evil, and madness is in their hearts during life; and afterward – to the dead!

Ecclesiastes 9:2-3

The LORD looked with favor on Abel and his offering, but on Cain and his offering he did not look with favor. So Cain was very angry and dejected. Then the LORD said to Cain: Why are you angry? Why are you dejected? If you act rightly, you will be accepted; but if not, sin lies in wait at the door; its urge is for you, yet you can rule over it."

Genesis 4:5-7

You speak as foolish women do. We accept good things from God; should we not accept evil?

Job 2:10

Is it not at the word of the Most High that both good and bad take place? What should the living complain about? About their sins! Let us search and examine our ways and return to the LORD!

Lamentations 3:38

You have heard that it was said, 'You shall love your neighbor and hate your enemy.' But I say to you, love your enemies, and pray for those who persecute you, that you may be children of your heavenly Father, for he makes his sun rise on the bad and the good, and causes rain to fall on the just and the unjust.

Matthew 5:43-45

"Lead us not into temptation, but deliver us from evil."

Matthew 6:13

Either declare the tree good and its fruit is good or declare the tree rotten and its fruit is rotten, for a tree is known by its fruit. You brood of vipers, how can you say good things when you are evil? For from the fullness of the heart the mouth speaks. A good person brings forth good out of a store of goodness, but an evil person brings evil out of a store of evil. I tell you, on the day of judgment people will render an account for every careless word they speak. By your words you will be acquitted and by your words you will be condemned.

Matthew 12: 33-37

Amen, I say to you, whatever you bind on earth shall be bound in heaven, and whatever you loose on earth shall be loosed in heaven."

Matthew 18:18

Toward the faithful you are faithful; to the honest man you are honest. Toward the pure, you are pure; but to the perverse you are devious. For humble people you save; haughty eyes you bring low.

Psalm 18:26-29

"The spirit of the LORD had departed from Saul, and he was tormented by an evil spirit from the LORD. So the servants of Saul said to him:"Look! An evil spirit from God is tormenting you. If your lordship will order it, we your servants here attending to you, will look for a man skilled in playing the harp. When the evil spirit from God comes upon you, he will play and you will feel better." Saul then told his servants, "Find me a good harpist and bring him to me." One of the servants spoke up: "I have observed that a son of Jesse of Bethlehem is a skillful harpist. He is also a brave warrior, an able speaker, and a handsome man. The LORD is certainly with him."

I Samuel 16:14-18

Toward the faithful you are faithful; to the honest you are honest; Toward the sincere you are sincere; but to the perverse you are devious. Humble people you save, though on the haughty your eyes look down.

II Samuel 22:26-28

Do not say, "His mercy is great; my many sins he will forgive. For mercy and anger alike are with him; his wrath comes to rest on the wicked."

Sirach 5:6

God in the beginning created human beings and made them subject to their own free choice. If you choose, you can keep the commandments; loyalty is doing the will of God. Set before you are fire and water; to whatever you choose, stretch out your hand. Before everyone are life and death, whichever they choose will be given them.

Sirach 15:14-17

Why is one day more important than another, when the same sun lights up every day of the year? ... As evil contrasts with good, and death with life, so are sinners in contrast with the godly. See now all the works of the Most High, they come in pairs, one the opposite of the other.

Sirach 33:7-15

At all times bless the Lord, your God, and ask him that all your paths may be straight and all your endeavors and plans may prosper. For no other nation possesses good counsel, but it is the Lord who gives all good things. Whomever the Lord chooses to raise is raised; and whomever the Lord chooses to cast down is cast down to the recesses of Hades. So now, son, keep in mind these my commandments, and never let them be erased from your heart.

APPENDIX II

And these are my orders for all the churches.
(1 Corinthians 7:18)

Paul's Dos and Don'ts

1.   Do not use sharp words towards someone of authority in the church. Rather, talk to them as you would to a father or mother and to the younger men and women, as you would to a brother or sister. (1 Timothy 5:1-2)

2.   Honor widows. (1 Timothy 5:3)

3.   It is good for men to have nothing to do with women but since the desires of the flesh give them   no choice, then every man should have a wife and every woman her husband. (1 Corinthians 7:1-2)

4.   It is good for the widowed and unmarried to be like Paul, but if they cannot be like him due to overwhelming desire, then they should get married. (1 Corinthians 7:7-9)

5.   A woman cannot divorce her husband. If she does, she is to remain unmarried or get back with her husband. (1 Corinthians 7:11)

6.   A man cannot divorce his wife. (1 Corinthians 7:11)

7.   If a member of the church is married to a non-Christian and he/she wants to remain with him then he should remain with her. (1 Corinthians 7:12-13)

8.   If a member of the church is married to a non-Christian and he/she does not want to remain in the marriage, then let them go and live with one another in peace. (1 Corinthians 7:12-13)

9.   A widow without family should pray day and night and if one gives herself over to pleasure is as good as dead. (1 Timothy 5:5)

10.   A woman is not to be considered a widow if she is under sixty and only married once. (1 Timothy 5:9)

11.　　Younger widows should be married so that they cannot go from house to house talking foolishness and saying things they have no right to say. (1 Timothy 5:11-14)

12.　　If a woman of faith has a friendship with a widow, she is to give her help so that the responsibility for care does not fall on the church. (1 Timothy 5:16)

13.　　Rulers who rule well should be doubly blessed, especially if their work is teaching and preaching. (1 Timothy 5:17)

14.　　Do not believe any allegation made against a person in authority unless there are two or three other people who testify to its truth. (1 Timothy 5:19)

15.　　Vilify sinners in public so that it puts fear in the hearts of anyone else who may think about sinning. (1 Timothy 5:20)

16.　　Do not lay hands on any man without thinking about it first. (1 Timothy 5:22)

17.　　Have no part in another man's sins. (1 Timothy 5:22)

18.　　Combine a little wine with the water you drink in order to keep your stomach in good health. (1　　　Timothy 5:23)

19.　　Slaves should honor their masters in order not to give their masters reason to think ill of God and his teachings. (1 Timothy 6:1)

20.　　If the master and slave are both of the faith, then the slave should have even more respect for the master and work even harder for him because they are brothers. (1 Timothy 6:2)

21.　　Men should pray. (1 Timothy 2:8)

22.　　If any man has been circumcised, let him remain so. And if any man who is a Christian and has not been circumcised, let him remain so. (1 Corinthians 7:18)

23.　　Women should dress simply with a sense of quiet and seriousness;

meaning no fancy hairdos, gold, jewels or expensive clothing. (1 Timothy 2:9)

24.   Women should do good works. (1 Timothy 2:10)

25.   A woman should place herself in the position of a learner who is under the authority of those more learned. (1 Timothy 2:11)

26.   Women should not be teachers. (1 Timothy 2:12)

27.   Women should be quiet and never have rule over a man. (1 Timothy 2:12)

28.   Women are to be serious in their behavior, saying nothing evil of others and controlling themselves by being true in all things. (1 Timothy 3:11)

29.   We instruct you, brothers, in the name of [our] Lord Jesus Christ, to shun any brother who conducts himself in a disorderly way and not according to the tradition they received from us. For you know how one must imitate us. (2 Thessalonians 3:6-7)

30.   Avoid foolish arguments, genealogies, rivalries, and quarrels about the law, for they are useless and futile. After a first and second warning, break off contact with a heretic, realizing that such a person is perverted and sinful and stands self-condemned.

30.   A bishop in the church is to
- have a good reputation,
- be married to only one woman,
- be self controlled,
- be respectful of order
- be serious,
- be a willing teacher,
- be hospitable to guests,
- not be quick to anger,
- not be a fighter,
- not be a lover of money,
- rule his house well
- keep his children under control,

- have been a member of the church for awhile,
- have a good name among those outside the church

(1 Timothy 3:2-7)

31.   A deacon in the church is to
- be serious-minded,
- be honest,
- be a moderate drinker,
- not greatly desire monetary wealth,
- be married to only one woman,
- rule his children and houses well,
- keep the secret of the faith in a sin-free heart, (1 Timothy 3:8-10)

32.   Old men are to
- be simple in their tastes,
- be serious,
- be wise,
- be true in faith,
- be loving
- be of a quiet mind. (Titus 2:2)

33.   Old women are to
- respect themselves in their behavior, which means they are not to gossip or drink too much wine and teach others that which is good. (Titus 2:3)
- teach the younger women to love their husbands and children,
- be wise in mind,
- be clean in heart,
- be kind,
- be homemakers,
- submit to the authority of their husbands. (Titus 2:3-5)

34.   Young men are to
- be wise and serious-minded,
- be an example of good works

- be holy in their teaching,
- be serious in their behavior,
- be honest. (Titus 2:6-8)

35. Servants are to
- be under the authority of their masters, doing what is pleasing to them without argument,
- not take what is not theirs

36. If you were a servant when you became a Christian, be happy with your situation; but if you have the chance to become free, make use of it. (1 Corinthians 7:21)

37. Servants are to do what their masters tell them, having respect and fear for them as they do of Christ. (Ephesians 6:5)

38. Masters are not to use violent words against their servants, in the knowledge that the master of both is in heaven. (Ephesians 6:9)

39. Be strong in the Lord and in the strength of his power. (Ephesians 6:10)

40. Paul has no orders from Jesus regarding virgins, but his own opinion as one whom Jesus has given his trust to, is that men should remain so. (1 Corinthians 7:26)

41. If married to a wife, do not leave her but if free of your wife, do not take another. (1 Corinthians 7:27)

42. Getting married is not a sin. Although those who do get married will have trouble in the flesh, Paul will not be hard on them. (1 Corinthians 7:28)

43. Those who have wives should act as they would if they did not have them. (1 Corinthians 7:29)

44. For those who are glad, give no signs of joy. (1 Corinthians 7:30)

45. For those who are sorrowful, give no signs of it. (1 Corinthians 7:30)

46.   For those who have property, act like you have nothing. (1 Corinthians 7:30)

47.   When a husband dies, a woman may remarry as long as long as she marries a Christian. But it is Paul's opinion since it "seems to him that he has the Spirit of God" that it would be better for her to remain unmarried. (1 Corinthians 7:39-40)

48.   Wives are to remain under the rule of their husbands in all things. (Ephesians 5:24)

49.   Husbands should have love for their wives. (Ephesians 5:28)

50.   There is to be no bad behavior or foolish talk. Replace foolish words with words of praise. (Ephesians 5:4)

51.   Children do what your mothers and fathers order. (Ephesians 6:1)

52.   Fathers are not to make their children angry. Rather, they are to train them in the teaching and fear of the Lord. (Ephesians 6:4)

BIBLIOGRAPHY
[Unless other wise indicated, all verses quoted from the Bible are from
The New American Bible, St. Joseph Edition]

1 Hitler, Adolf. Mein Kampf (Kindle Locations 1159-1167). Unknown. Kindle Edition.

2 Ibid. (Locations 1167-1175).

3 Ibid. (Location 1182).

4 Ibid. (Location 245).

5 Ibid. (Kindle Location 452).

6 Carruthers, Bob. The Nuremberg Trials - The Complete Proceedings Vol 10: The Case against von   Ribbentrop (The Third Reich from Original Sources) (Kindle Locations 4982-4986). Coda Books Ltd. Kindle Edition.

7 Hitler, Adolf. Mein Kampf (Kindle Location 515). Unknown. Kindle Edition.

8 Ibid. (Locations 775-776).

9 Ibid. (Locations 798-802).

10 Ibid. (Location 805).

11 Ibid. (Locations 811-818).

12 Ibid. (Kindle Locations 847-853).

13 Ibid. (Locations 846-872).

14 Carruthers, Bob (2011-11-13). The Nuremberg Trials - The Complete Proceedings Vol 4: Individual Responsibility of the Defendants (The Third Reich from Original Sources) (Locations 1707-1709). Coda Books

Ltd. Kindle Edition.

15 Hitler, Adolf. Mein Kampf (Location 862). Unknown. Kindle Edition.

16 "Soon We Won't Program Computers. We'll Train Them Like Dogs," Edward C. Monaghan, https://www.wired.com/2016/05/the-end-of-code/

17 Shirer, William. The Rise and Fall of the Third Reich (p. 326). Rosetta Books. Kindle Edition.

18 Ibid. (p. 347).

19 Carruthers, Bob. The Nuremberg Trials - The Complete Proceedings Vol 3: The Policy to Exterminate the Jews (The Third Reich from Original Sources) (Kindle Locations 3081-3091). Coda Books Ltd. Kindle Edition.

20 Ibid.

21 Carruthers, Bob. The Nuremberg Trials - The Complete Proceedings Vol. 1: The Indictment and Opening Statements (The Third Reich from Original Sources) (Locations 1710-1726). Coda Books Ltd. Kindle Edition.

22 Ibid. (Locations 227-237).

23 Shirer, William. The Rise and Fall of the Third Reich (p. 577). Rosetta Books. Kindle Edition.

24 Carruthers, Bob. The Nuremberg Trials - The Complete Proceedings Vol 9: The Case against Goering (The Third Reich from Original Sources) (Kindle Locations 2513-2517). Coda Books Ltd. Kindle Edition.

25 Carruthers, Bob. The Nuremberg Trials - The Complete Proceedings Vol 3: The Policy to Exterminate the Jews (The Third Reich from Original Sources) (Kindle Locations 4386-4388). Coda Books Ltd. Kindle Edition.

26 Ibid. (Kindle Locations 2692-2697).

27 Shirer, William. The Rise and Fall of the Third Reich (p. 326). Rosetta Books. Kindle Edition; Shirer, William. The Rise and Fall of the Third Reich (p. 347). Rosetta Books. Kindle Edition.

28 Ibid. (p. 111).

29 Hare, Robert, Phd. (1999) Without Conscience; The Disturbing World of the Psychopaths Among Us. The Guilford Press, a Division of Guilford Publications, Inc.

30 Shirer, William. The Rise and Fall of the Third Reich (p. 247-248). Rosetta Books. Kindle Edition.

31 Hitler, Adolf. Mein Kampf (Kindle Locations 2931-2962). Unknown. Kindle Edition.

32 Ibid. (Kindle Locations 2954-2962).

33 Ibid. (Kindle Locations 2948-2951).

34Carruthers, Bob. The Nuremberg Trials - The Complete Proceedings Vol 2: The Indictment - the Four Charges (The Third Reich from Original Sources) (Kindle Locations 7544-7545). Coda Books Ltd. Kindle Edition.

35 Wikipedia, https://en.wikipedia.org/wiki/Hans_Fritzsche.

36 Carruthers, Bob. The Nuremberg Trials - The Complete Proceedings Vol 3: The Policy to Exterminate the Jews (The Third Reich from Original Sources) (Kindle Locations 2679-2693). Coda Books Ltd. Kindle Edition.

37 Carruthers, Bob. The Nuremberg Trials - The Complete Proceedings Vol 5: The Concentration Camps (The Third Reich from Original Sources) (Kindle Locations 2488-2509). Coda Books Ltd. Kindle Edition.

38 Ibid. (Kindle Locations 2466-2509).

39 Ibid. (Kindle Locations 2585-2593).

40 Ibid. (Kindle Locations 2596-2601).

41 Shirer, William. The Rise and Fall of the Third Reich (p. 349). RosettaBooks. Kindle Edition.

42 Shirer, William. The Rise and Fall of the Third Reich (p. 111). Rosetta Books. Kindle Edition.

43 Kershaw, Alex (2010-10-26). The Envoy: The Epic Rescue of the Last Jews of Europe in the Desperate Closing Months of World War II (pp. 204-205). Perseus Books Group. Kindle Edition.

44 https://www.britannica.com/topic/Einsatzstab-Reichsleiter-Rosenberg

45 The Nuremberg Trials - The Complete Proceedings Vol 6: Occupation, Propaganda and the Russian Camps (The Third Reich from Original Sources) (Kindle Locations 3128-3147). Coda Books Ltd. Kindle Edition.

46 Carruthers, Bob. The Nuremberg Trials - The Complete Proceedings Vol 2: The Indictment - the Four Charges (The Third Reich from Original Sources) (Kindle Locations 7429-7437). Coda Books Ltd. Kindle Edition.

47 Carruthers, Bob. The Nuremberg Trials - The Complete Proceedings Vol 2: The Indictment - the Four Charges (The Third Reich from Original Sources) (Kindle Locations 10572-10576). Coda Books Ltd. Kindle Edition.

48 Ibid. (Kindle Locations 10579-10582).

49 Carruthers, Bob. The Nuremberg Trials - The Complete Proceedings Vol 9: The Case against Goering (The Third Reich from Original Sources) (Kindle Locations 2662-2677). Coda Books Ltd. Kindle Edition.

50 Carruthers, Bob. The Nuremberg Trials - The Complete Proceedings Vol 2: The Indictment - the Four Charges (The Third Reich from Original Sources) (Kindle Locations 10579-10582). Coda Books Ltd. Kindle Edition.

51 Psychiatric distress and symptoms of PTSD among victims of bullying at work, STIG BERGE MATTHIESEN & STALE EINARSEN, Division of Work and Organisational Psychology, Department of Psychosocial Science, University of Bergen, Christiesgate 12, N-5015 Bergen, Norway.

52 Carruthers, Bob. The Nuremberg Trials - The Complete Proceedings Vol 4: Individual Responsibility of the Defendants (The Third Reich from Original Sources) (Kindle Locations 1419-1438). Coda Books Ltd. Kindle Edition.

53 Carruthers, Bob. The Nuremberg Trials - The Complete Proceedings Vol 3: The Policy to Exterminate the Jews (The Third Reich from Original Sources) (Kindle Locations 4017-4022). Coda Books Ltd. Kindle Edition.

54 Shirer, William. The Rise and Fall of the Third Reich (p. 937-938). RosettaBooks. Kindle Edition.

55 Mobbing: At the Mercy of the Mob, A Summary of Research on Workplace Mobbing, Prof. Kenneth Westhues, University of Waterloo, overcomebullying.org./mobbing-bullying-research.html.

56 Mobbing in the Workplace: Even the Good Go Bad, http://www.huffingtonpost.com/janice-harper/mobbing-in-the-workplace-_b_1102815.html, Posted: 11/23/11 09:12 AM ET, Janice Harper, Anthroplogist.

57 Mobbing and Psychological Terror at Workplaces, Heinz Leymann, Ph.D., University of Stockholm and National Institute of Occupational Health, Stockholm, Sweden, Violence and Victims, Vol. 5, No. 2, 1990, Springer Publishing Company.

58 Carruthers, Bob. The Nuremberg Trials - The Complete Proceedings Vol 5: The Concentration Camps (The Third Reich from Original Sources) (Kindle Locations 7991-7995). Coda Books Ltd. Kindle Edition.

59 Shirer, William. The Rise and Fall of the Third Reich (p. 203). Rosetta Books. Kindle Edition.

60 Carruthers, Bob. The Nuremberg Trials - The Complete Proceedings Vol 6: The Concentration Camps (The Third Reich from Original Sources) (Kindle Locations 2469-2478). Coda Books Ltd. Kindle Edition.

61 Shirer, William. The Rise and Fall of the Third Reich (p. 232-234). Rosetta Books. Kindle Edition.

62 Carruthers, Bob. The Nuremberg Trials - The Complete Proceedings Vol 4: Individual Responsibility of the Defendants (The Third Reich from Original Sources) (Kindle Locations 12546-12557). Coda Books Ltd. Kindle Edition.

63 Carruthers, Bob. The Nuremberg Trials - The Complete Proceedings Vol 5: The Concentration Camps (The Third Reich from Original Sources) (Kindle Locations 7991-7995). Coda Books Ltd. Kindle Edition.

64 Carruthers, Bob. The Nuremberg Trials - The Complete Proceedings Vol 2: The Indictment - the Four Charges (The Third Reich from Original Sources) (Kindle Locations 11238-11240). Coda Books Ltd. Kindle

Edition.

65 Hitler, Adolf. Mein Kampf (Kindle Locations 5179-5180). Unknown. Kindle Edition.

66 The Nuremberg Trials - The Complete Proceedings Vol 6: Occupation, Propaganda and the Russian Camps (The Third Reich from Original Sources) (Kindle Locations 6093-6095). Coda Books Ltd. Kindle Edition.

67 Hitler, Adolf (2012-07-28). Mein Kampf. Kindle Edition.

68 Carruthers, Bob. The Nuremberg Trials - The Complete Proceedings Vol 10: The Case against von Ribbentrop (The Third Reich from Original Sources) (Kindle Locations 2707-2714). Coda Books Ltd. Kindle Edition.

69 Ibid. (Kindle Locations 2656-2664).

70 Ibid. (Kindle Locations 2685-2689).

71 Carruthers, Bob. The Nuremberg Trials - The Complete Proceedings Vol 4: Individual Responsibility of the Defendants (The Third Reich from Original Sources) (Kindle Locations 2066-2070). Coda Books Ltd. Kindle Edition.

72 Shirer, William. (2011-10-23) The Rise and Fall of the Third Reich (p. 86). Rosetta Books. Kindle Edition.

73 Shirer, William. The Rise and Fall of the Third Reich (p. 322). Rosetta Books. Kindle Edition.

74 Carruthers, Bob. The Nuremberg Trials - The Complete Proceedings Vol 3: The Policy to Exterminate the Jews (The Third Reich from Original Sources) . Coda Books Ltd. Kindle Edition.

75 Ibid. (Kindle Locations 343-371).

76 Shirer, William. The Rise and Fall of the Third Reich (p. 434). Rosetta Books. Kindle Edition.

77 Carruthers, Bob. The Nuremberg Trials - The Complete Proceedings Vol 11: The Case against Kaltenbrunner (The Third Reich from Original Sources) (Kindle Locations 11400-11409). Coda Books Ltd. Kindle Edition.

78 Kershaw, Alex (2010-10-26). The Envoy: The Epic Rescue of the Last Jews of Europe in the Desperate Closing Months of World War II (p. 39). Perseus Books Group. Kindle Edition.

79 Carruthers, Bob. The Nuremberg Trials - The Complete Proceedings Vol 11: The Case against Kaltenbrunner (The Third Reich from Original Sources) (Kindle Locations 7881-7889). Coda Books Ltd. Kindle Edition.

80 Ibid. (Kindle Locations 11468-11480).

81 Carruthers, Bob. The Nuremberg Trials - The Complete Proceedings Vol 2: The Indictment - the Four Charges (The Third Reich from Original Sources) (Locations 5292-5297, 6112-6116). Coda Books Ltd. Kindle Edition.

82 Carruthers, Bob. The Nuremberg Trials - The Complete Proceedings Vol 10: The Case against von Ribbentrop (The Third Reich from Original Sources) (Locations 1723-1725). Coda Books Ltd. Kindle Edition.

83 Carruthers, Bob. The Nuremberg Trials - The Complete Proceedings Vol 3: The Policy to Exterminate the Jews (The Third Reich from Original Sources) (Locations 7676-7690). Coda Books Ltd. Kindle Edition.

84 The Nuremberg Trials - The Complete Proceedings Vol 6: Occupation, Propaganda and the Russian Camps (The Third Reich from Original Sources) (Locations 2765-2833). Coda Books Ltd. Kindle Edition.

85 https://en.wikipedia.org/wiki/Reichstag_Fire_Decree.

86 Ibid. (Kindle Locations 10557--10567).

87 Carruthers, Bob. The Nuremberg Trials - The Complete Proceedings Vol 4: Individual Responsibility of the Defendants (The Third Reich from Original Sources) (Kindle Locations 1707-1709). Coda Books Ltd. Kindle Edition.

88 Carruthers, Bob. The Nuremberg Trials - The Complete Proceedings Vol 2: The Indictment - the Four Charges (The Third Reich from Original Sources) (Kindle Locations 10579-10582). Coda Books Ltd. Kindle Edition.

89 Carruthers, Bob. The Nuremberg Trials - The Complete Proceedings Vol 2: The Indictment - the Four Charges (The Third Reich from Original Sources) (Kindle Locations 10557--10567). Coda Books Ltd. Kindle Edition.

90 Carruthers, Bob. The Nuremberg Trials - The Complete Proceedings Vol 2: The Indictment - the Four Charges (The Third Reich from Original Sources) (Kindle Locations 219-225). Coda Books Ltd. Kindle Edition; Bob Carruthers. The Nuremberg Trials - The Complete Proceedings Vol 10: The Case against von Ribbentrop (The Third Reich from Original Sources) (Kindle Locations 1723-1725). Coda Books Ltd. Kindle Edition.

91 Shirer, William. The Rise and Fall of the Third Reich (p. 518-520). RosettaBooks. Kindle Edition; Carruthers, Bob. The Nuremberg Trials - The Complete Proceedings Vol 3: The Policy to Exterminate the Jews (The Third Reich from Original Sources) (Kindle Locations 5815-5823). Coda Books Ltd. Kindle Edition.

92 Carruthers, Bob. The Nuremberg Trials - The Complete Proceedings Vol 11: The Case against Kaltenbrunner (The Third Reich from Original Sources) (Locations 713-723). Coda Books Ltd. Kindle Edition.

93 Ibid. (Location 7855).

94 Carruthers, Bob. The Nuremberg Trials - The Complete Proceedings Vol 5: The Concentration Camps (The Third Reich from Original Sources) (Kindle Locations 7807-7809). Coda Books Ltd. Kindle Edition.

95 Carruthers, Bob. The Nuremberg Trials - The Complete Proceedings Vol 11: The Case against Kaltenbrunner (The Third Reich from Original Sources) (Kindle Locations 713-723). Coda Books Ltd. Kindle Edition.

96 Kershaw, Alex (2010-10-26). The Envoy: The Epic Rescue of the Last Jews of Europe in the Desperate Closing Months of World War II (pp. 205-206). Perseus Books Group. Kindle Edition.

97 Shirer, William (2011-10-23). The Rise and Fall of the Third Reich (pp. 661-662). Rosetta Books. Kindle Edition.

98 Ibid. (p. 146).

99 Carruthers, Bob. The Nuremberg Trials - The Complete Proceedings Vol 4: Individual Responsibility of the Defendants (The Third Reich from

Original Sources) (Kindle Locations 2273-2286). Coda Books Ltd. Kindle Edition.

100 Carruthers, Bob. The Nuremberg Trials - The Complete Proceedings Vol 4: Individual Responsibility of the Defendants (The Third Reich from Original Sources) (Kindle Locations 2273-2286). Coda Books Ltd. Kindle Edition.

101 Carruthers, Bob. The Nuremberg Trials - The Complete Proceedings Vol 11: The Case against Kaltenbrunner (The Third Reich from Original Sources) (Kindle Locations 711-713). Coda Books Ltd. Kindle Edition.

102 Ibid. (pp. 226-227).

103 Bob Carruthers. The Nuremberg Trials - The Complete Proceedings Vol 11: The Case against Kaltenbrunner (The Third Reich from Original Sources) (Kindle Locations 11468-11480). Coda Books Ltd. Kindle Edition; Vol 9: The Case against Goering (The Third Reich from Original Sources) (Kindle Locations 1422-1429). Coda Books Ltd. Kindle Edition; Vol 10: The Case against von Ribbentrop (The Third Reich from Original Sources) (Kindle Locations 10489-10506). Coda Books Ltd. Kindle Edition and Vol 5: The Concentration Camps (The Third Reich from Original Sources) (Kindle Locations 7788-7790). Coda Books Ltd. Kindle Edition.

104 Shirer, William (2011-10-23). The Rise and Fall of the Third Reich (p. 227). Rosetta Books. Kindle Edition.

105 Hitler, Adolf. Mein Kampf (Kindle Location 6048). Unknown. Kindle Edition.

106 Shirer, William. The Rise and Fall of the Third Reich (p. 88). RosettaBooks. Kindle Edition.

107 Hitler, Adolf. Mein Kampf (Kindle Location 1685). Unknown. Kindle Edition.

108 Shirer, William.The Rise and Fall of the Third Reich (pp. 89-90). Rosetta Books. Kindle Edition.

109 Ibid. (p. 120).

110 Bob Carruthers. The Nuremberg Trials - The Complete Proceedings Vol 5: The Concentration Camps (The Third Reich from Original Sources) (Kindle Locations 9595-9597). Coda Books Ltd. Kindle Edition.

111 Bob Carruthers. The Nuremberg Trials - The Complete Proceedings Vol 10: The Case against von Ribbentrop (The Third Reich from Original Sources) (Kindle Locations 2732-2733). Coda Books Ltd. Kindle Edition.

112 Wikipedia, https://en.wikipedia.org/wiki/Sicherheitsdienst

113 Carruthers, Bob. The Nuremberg Trials - The Complete Proceedings Vol 3: The Policy to Exterminate the Jews (The Third Reich from Original Sources) (Kindle Locations 5766-6709). Coda Books Ltd. Kindle Edition.

114 Carruthers, Bob. The Nuremberg Trials - The Complete Proceedings Vol 9: The Case against Goering (The Third Reich from Original Sources) (Kindle Locations 2763-2766). Coda Books Ltd. Kindle Edition.

115 Carruthers, Bob. The Nuremberg Trials - The Complete Proceedings Vol 11: The Case against Kaltenbrunner (The Third Reich from Original Sources) (Kindle Locations 5096-5099). Coda Books Ltd. Kindle Edition.

116 Carruthers, Bob. The Nuremberg Trials - The Complete Proceedings Vol 3: The Policy to Exterminate the Jews (The Third Reich from Original Sources) (Kindle Locations 3350 - 3351). Coda Books Ltd. Kindle Edition.

117 Carruthers, Bob. The Nuremberg Trials - The Complete Proceedings Vol 3: The Policy to Exterminate the Jews (The Third Reich from Original Sources) (Kindle Locations 489-491). Coda Books Ltd. Kindle Edition; Shirer, William. The Rise and Fall of the Third Reich (p. 126). Rosetta Books. Kindle Edition; Shirer, William. The Rise and Fall of the Third Reich (pp. 143-144). Rosetta Books. Kindle Edition.

118 Carruthers, Bob. The Nuremberg Trials - The Complete Proceedings Vol 3: The Policy to Exterminate the Jews (The Third Reich from Original Sources) (Kindle Locations 489-491). Coda Books Ltd. Kindle.

119 Shirer, William. The Rise and Fall of the Third Reich (pp. 59-60). Rosetta Books. Kindle Edition.

120 Carruthers, Bob. The Nuremberg Trials - The Complete Proceedings Vol 5: The Concentration Camps (The Third Reich from Original Sources) (Kindle Location 981-986). Coda Books Ltd. Kindle Edition.

121 Carruthers, Bob. The Nuremberg Trials - The Complete Proceedings Vol 2: The Indictment - the Four Charges (The Third Reich from Original Sources) (Kindle Locations 8642-8644). Coda Books Ltd. Kindle Edition.

122 Carruthers, Bob. The Nuremberg Trials - The Complete Proceedings Vol 10: The Case against von Ribbentrop (The Third Reich from Original Sources) (Kindle Locations 9312-9314). Coda Books Ltd. Kindle Edition.

123 Carruthers, Bob. The Nuremberg Trials - The Complete Proceedings Vol 2: The Indictment - the Four Charges (The Third Reich from Original Sources) (Kindle Locations 7176-7186). Coda Books Ltd. Kindle Edition.

124 Carruthers, Bob. The Nuremberg Trials - The Complete Proceedings Vol 5: The Concentration Camps (The Third Reich from Original Sources) (Kindle Locations 758-763). Coda Books Ltd. Kindle Edition.

125 Carruthers, Bob. The Nuremberg Trials - The Complete Proceedings Vol 4: Individual Responsibility of the Defendants (The Third Reich from Original Sources) (Kindle Locations 4542-4547). Coda Books Ltd. Kindle Edition.

126 Ibid. (Kindle Locations 12132-12140).

127 Carruthers, Bob. The Nuremberg Trials - The Complete Proceedings Vol 4: Individual Responsibility of the Defendants (The Third Reich from Original Sources) (Kindle Locations 12132-12140). Coda Books Ltd. Kindle Edition; Bob Carruthers. The Nuremberg Trials - The Complete Proceedings Vol 10: The Case against von Ribbentrop (The Third Reich from Original Sources) (Kindle Locations 1721-1723). Coda Books Ltd. Kindle Edition.

128 Carruthers, Bob. The Nuremberg Trials - The Complete Proceedings Vol 3: The Policy to Exterminate the Jews (The Third Reich from Original Sources) (Kindle Locations 212-232). Coda Books Ltd. Kindle Edition.

129 The Nuremberg Trials - The Complete Proceedings Vol: 1 The Indictment and Opening Statements (The Third Reich from Original Sources) (Kindle Locations 594-611). Coda Books Ltd. Kindle Edition.

130 Carruthers, Bob. The Nuremberg Trials - The Complete Proceedings Vol 2: The Indictment - the Four Charges (The Third Reich from Original

Sources) (Kindle Locations 10596-10606). Coda Books Ltd. Kindle Edition.

131 Ibid. (Kindle Locations 10618-10623).

132 Carruthers, Bob. The Nuremberg Trials - The Complete Proceedings Vol 5: The Concentration Camps (The Third Reich from Original Sources) (Kindle Locations 8358-8361). Coda Books Ltd. Kindle Edition; Bob Carruthers. The Nuremberg Trials - The Complete Proceedings Vol 9: The Concentration Camps (The Third Reich from Original Sources) (Kindle Locations 425-432; Bob Carruthers. The Nuremberg Trials - The Complete Proceedings Vol 3. The Concentration Camps (The Third Reich from Original Sources) (Kindle Locations 5766-5772). Coda Books Ltd. Kindle Edition.). Coda Books Ltd. Kindle Edition.

133 Carruthers, Bob. The Nuremberg Trials - The Complete Proceedings Vol 3: The Policy to Exterminate the Jews (The Third Reich from Original Sources) (Kindle Locations 7140-7144). Coda Books Ltd. Kindle Edition.

134 Carruthers, Bob. The Nuremberg Trials - The Complete Proceedings Vol 2: The Indictment - the Four Charges (The Third Reich from Original Sources) (Kindle Locations 10557-10558). Coda Books Ltd. Kindle Edition.

135 Ibid. (Kindle Locations 11103-11106).

136 Carruthers, Bob. The Nuremberg Trials - The Complete Proceedings Vol 10: The Case against von Ribbentrop (The Third Reich from Original Sources) (Kindle Locations 2718-2725). Coda Books Ltd. Kindle Edition.

137 The Nuremberg Trials - The Complete Proceedings Vol: 1 The Indictment and Opening Statements (The Third Reich from Original Sources) (Kindle Locations 2065-2067). Coda Books Ltd. Kindle Edition

138 Ibid. (Kindle Location 2050-2054).

139 Hitler, Adolf. Mein Kampf, Loc. 815.

140 Ibid. Loc. 1121.260.

141 Ibid. Loc. 976.

142 Ibid. Locs. 1042-1055.

143 Ibid. 1071.

144 Ibid. Locs. 1100-1104.

145 Ibid. Locs. 1125-1129.

146 Ibid. Loc. 1186.

147 John 11:45-53.

148 John. The Official King James Bible Online, Authorized Version (KJV). N.p., n.d. Web. 23 Mar. 2014.
<http://www.kingjamesbibleonline.org/book.php?
book=John&chapter=11&verse=49-50>.

149 John 12:10-11.

150 Luke 7:36.

151 "Motive." *The Free Dictionary by Farlex*. N.p., n.d. Web. 24 Mar. 2014.
<http://legal-dictionary.thefreedictionary.com>

152 Matthew. The Official King James Bible Online, Authorized Version (KJV). N.p., n.d. Web. 24 Mar. 2014.
<http://www.kingjamesbibleonline.org/book.php?
book=Matthew&chapter=15&verse=17-19>. "17 Do not ye yet understand, that whatsoever entereth in at the mouth goeth into the belly, and is cast out into the draught? 18 But those things which proceed out of the mouth come forth from the heart; and they defile the man. 19 For out of the heart proceed evil thoughts, murders, adulteries, fornications, thefts, false witness, blasphemies."

153 Wake, William (2012-05-17). Forbidden books of the original New Testament (pp. 87-88). Kindle Edition.

154 Carruthers, Bob. The Nuremberg Trials - The Complete Proceedings Vol 2: The Indictment - the Four Charges (The Third Reich from Original Sources) (Kindle Locations 10557--10567). Coda Books Ltd. Kindle Edition.

155 John 7:19-20.

156 Mark 12:1-12, Luke 20:9-18.

157 Wake, William (2012-05-17). Forbidden books of the original New Testament (pp. 103-104). Kindle Edition.

158 Giang, Vivian. "Barely Legal Things Employers Do To Keep Unemployed Applicants Out." *Yahoo Finance.* N.p., 17 July 2013. Web. 21 Mar. 2014. <http://finance.yahoo.com/news/barely-legal-things-employers-keep-190600487.html>

159 Matthew 12:22-31.

160 Genesis 3:24.

161 Hitler, Adolf. Mein Kampf (Kindle Location 6049). Unknown. Kindle Edition.

162 Ibid. (Kindle Locations 7136-7140).

163 Carruthers, Bob (2011-11-13). The Nuremberg Trials - The Complete Proceedings Vol 4: Individual Responsibility of the Defendants (The Third Reich from Original Sources) (Kindle Locations 5342-5344). Coda Books Ltd. Kindle Edition.

164 Hitler, Adolf. Mein Kampf. (Kindle Locations 1121-1129). Unknown. Kindle Edition.

165 Wake, William (2012-05-17). Forbidden books of the original New Testament (p. 119-120). Kindle Edition.

166 Hall, Manly P.. The Secret Teachings of All Ages (p. 546). Start Publishing LLC. Kindle Edition.

167 Revelation 1:1-3

168 Johnson, Lisa. Patterns of Peter and Paul.

169 The Nag Hammadi library (also known as the "Gnostic Gospels") is a collection of early Christian and Gnostic texts discovered near the Upper Egyptian town of Nag Hammadi in 1945. https://en.wikipedia.org/wiki/Nag_Hammadi_library.

170 Fillmore, Charles. The Revealing Word - A Dictionary Of Metaphysical Terms (The Sacred Books Book 112) . Jazzybee Publishing.

Kindle Edition.

171 Wake, William (2012-05-17). Forbidden books of the original New Testament (pp. 87-88). Kindle Edition.

172 Wake, William (2012-05-17). The First Gospel of the Infancy of Jesus Christ. Forbidden books of the original New Testament (pp. 85-86). Kindle Edition.

173 Nyland, Dr A. (2011-06-13). The Gospel of Thomas (pp. 27-28). Unknown. Kindle Edition.

174 Genesis 3:21.

175 Fillmore, Charles. The Revealing Word - A Dictionary Of Metaphysical Terms (The Sacred Books Book 112) . Jazzybee Publishing. Kindle Edition.

176 Kershaw, Alex (2010-10-26). The Envoy: The Epic Rescue of the Last Jews of Europe in the Desperate Closing Months of World War II (pp. 204-205). Perseus Books Group. Kindle Edition.

177 Shirer, William. The Rise and Fall of the Third Reich (p. 226-227). RosettaBooks. Kindle Edition.

178 Carruthers, Bob (2011-11-13). The Nuremberg Trials - The Complete Proceedings Vol 4: Individual Responsibility of the Defendants (The Third Reich from Original Sources) (Kindle Locations 9441-9449). Coda Books Ltd. Kindle Edition.

179 John 16:13.

180 <http://answers.yahoo.com> (accessed February 25, 2012).

181 Matthew 23:27-28.

182 Luke 7:34.

www.ingramcontent.com/pod-product-compliance
Lightning Source LLC
Chambersburg PA
CBHW060448280326
41933CB00014B/2700